The Substitute Teacher's Guide to Success

Ellen L. Kronowitz

Professor Emerita

California State University, San Bernardino

Boston   Columbus   Indianapolis   New York   San Francisco   Upper Saddle River
Amsterdam   Cape Town   Dubai   London   Madrid   Milan   Munich   Paris   Montreal   Toronto
Delhi   Mexico City   Sao Paulo   Sydney   Hong Kong   Seoul   Singapore   Taipei   Tokyo

Vice President and Editor in Chief:
Jeffery W. Johnston
Acquisitions Editor: Meredith D. Fossel
Editorial Assistant: Nancy Holstein
Vice President, Director of Marketing:
Quinn Perkson
Senior Marketing Manager:
Darcy Betts Prybella
Senior Managing Editor:
Pamela Bennett
Senior Project Manager: Mary M. Irvin
Senior Operations Supervisor:
Matt Ottenweller

Senior Art Director: Diane Lorenzo
Cover Designer: Ali Mohrman
Cover Art: iStock
Permissions Administrator:
Rebecca Savage
Full-Service Project Management:
Thistle Hill Publishing Services, LLC
Composition: Integra Software Services

Text Font: Times

Every effort has been made to provide accurate and current Internet information in this book. However, the Internet and information posted on it are constantly changing, so it is inevitable that some of the Internet addresses listed in this textbook will change.

Library of Congress Cataloging-in-Publication Data

Kronowitz, Ellen L.
   The substitute teacher's guide to success / Ellen L. Kronowitz.
      p. cm.
   Includes bibliographical references and index.
   ISBN-13: 978-0-205-62495-9 (pbk.)
   ISBN-10: 0-205-62495-2 (pbk.)
   1. Substitute teachers—United States—Handbooks, manuals, etc.   I. Title.
LB2844.1.S8K76 2011
371.14'122—dc22

2010001487

www.pearsonhighered.com

ISBN 10:   0-205-62495-2
ISBN 13: 978-0-205-62495-9

This book is dedicated to hard-working substitute teachers,
stand-ins who save the day for learning
in classrooms far and wide.

ABOUT THE AUTHOR

Dr. Ellen Kronowitz has been an elementary and middle school teacher in urban as well as rural school districts. All of her advanced degrees are from Teachers College, Columbia University, where she taught at the Agnes Russell School, the university demonstration school. She is a Professor Emerita of Education at CSU, San Bernardino, where she taught social studies methods, graduate curriculum and instruction courses, and supervised student teachers and interns. She was the liaison to the Hillside-University Demonstration School, a partnership in its 23rd year. In addition to numerous conference presentations and journal articles, she has authored three books to help beginning teachers through their first years of teaching: *Beyond Student Teaching, Your First Year of Teaching and Beyond,* Fourth Edition, and her most recent, *The Teacher's Guide to Success.*

Letter from the Author

Hello, my name is Ellen Kronowitz, the author of *The Substitute Teacher's Guide to Success.*

Substitute teachers have a very important role in the educational community because they save the day for learning. They are team members in schools to ensure the continuity of instruction and, as such, have a chance to have an impact on the students they work with.

Whether you are a new substitute teacher or are considering becoming a substitute teacher, you may feel some apprehension about this new and different role, regardless of your preparation. The purpose of this guide is to help you feel more confident and prepared for substitute teaching.

There are challenges, and there will be obstacles that will get in the way of your efforts to substitute teach effectively. But along with those challenges come many individual joys and opportunities to develop your skills as a substitute teacher. In some cases, the students you encounter, the skills you learn, and the attitudes you develop will serve you well should you decide to take the next step into full-time teaching.

With each subbing assignment, you will delight in knowing that you have provided continuity for learning and have made a difference. The students you meet will expand your knowledge and skills, and the opportunity to substitute teach in different settings with diverse students, grade levels, and subject matter is invaluable. Most teachers who do not sub first would like to have experienced different grade levels and subject matter. No two classrooms are ever the same and no two subbing experiences are the same.

As years go by, you may not remember each and every student you encounter, but rest assured that they will remember you. "Hey, Grandma,

I am glad to see you back on campus," called out one high school student affectionately as I walked the campus with a very experienced teacher and now regular high school sub. She smiled back, and with a knowing smile, she knew she would always be "Grandma" in their mind's eye. While I cannot be there in the classroom with you, I believe you will find *The Substitute Teacher's Guide to Success* the next best thing.

Ellen Kronowitz

Preface

Substitute teachers are more than placeholders, entertainers, or babysitters. They are professionals on a team of educators who enable quality instruction to go forward in the regularly assigned teacher's absence. They provide continuity in the teacher's absence by effectively managing the classroom and successfully implementing the teacher's plans.

The Substitute Teacher's Guide to Success is a practical guidebook reflecting best practices within a standards-based educational system and focusing on topics that are essential to successful substitute teaching at elementary, middle, and high school levels. Since many states require no formal training for substitute teachers, and some states have minimal requirements for substitute teachers beyond a high school diploma, it is essential to have well-trained and qualified substitutes in the classroom.

In this age of NCLB, standards-based instruction, and Race to the Top, substitute teachers no longer can "do their own thing" and carry around a bag of tricks to amuse students. They need accurate information not only on how to get a job but, more important, to be able to envision what they will encounter in the classroom. And across the country, students, in the absence of their teacher, require and deserve highly trained and well-qualified substitute teachers. This book will be a quick and easy reference guide to professional content and advice for the substitute teacher.

Audience

This handbook was written for potential and novice substitute teachers in all regions and settings and at all grade levels, K–12. It is a quick and easy reference to help individuals make an informed decision to sub and to sustain and encourage them while they are in the induction phase of substitute teaching. Working subs may find ideas to invigorate their practice.

Supervisors, administrators, curriculum coordinators, mentor teachers, teachers, and substitute teaching coordinators will find that this handbook facilitates their work with new or continuing substitute teachers.

Content and Organization

The fifteen chapters and epilogue address the most practical aspects of substitute teaching. These chapters will simplify the complex challenges ahead. They will show how teachers prepare for subs and how subs apply for a subbing position, prepare for the first day of subbing, dress and behave professionally, begin the day, interpret lesson plans, follow teachers' routines, and determine the nature of the discipline plan in place. The chapters also provide some low-key discipline interventions to rely on, how to engage students in instruction, end the day, and take care of professional and personal needs. Chapter 15 provides a wealth of information and resources for use in preparing for subbing positions, including how to prepare for the prospect of finding no lesson plans to guide you.

Unique Features

The Substitute Teacher's Guide to Success contains a variety of unique features that will help readers make the most of this guide.

- **Effectiveness Essentials** at the beginning of each chapter outline the key concepts within the chapter.
- **Apply It!** activities provide ideas for the reader to work through with or without instructors.
- **Avoid It!** provides tips about mistakes substitute teachers should try to avoid.
- **Classroom Artifacts** provide lesson plans and instructions to subs that have been shared by practicing teachers and administrators, including substitute teaching handbooks.
- **Myth Busters!** dispel false yet prevalent notions.
- **Statistics** give an up-to-date look at substitute teaching.
- A series of features include quotes and shared stories from substitute teachers, veterans in the field, administrators, and students: **Principal's Perspective/Substitute Speaks/Teacher Talks . . .** are filled with anecdotes from experienced teachers, current substitute teachers, and administrators; **Student Says . . .** are reflections from students of all ages on substitute teaching and substitute teachers.
- The guide ends with **resources and Web sites** for more information.

Adapt the guidance in *The Substitute Teacher's Guide to Success* to your own circumstances and subject area. Use the resources provided to help identify, clarify, solidify, and/or modify your currently held beliefs about what constitutes an effective substitute teacher. Use this guide as your road map to successful substituting experiences.

ACKNOWLEDGMENTS

It takes a committed team of professionals to tend this project from start to finish, and I was fortunate to have the best. I would like to express my gratitude to Meredith Fossel, acquisitions editor in Foundations of Education and Counseling at Pearson. I relied throughout on her expertise and sound advice. To all of you at Pearson who helped along the way, especially Mary Irvin and Nancy Holstein, I offer my deep appreciation and heartfelt thanks. Thanks also to Angela Williams Urquhart at Thistle Hill Publishing Services.

I want to thank the following reviewers whose attention to the big picture as well as the details made this a much better book. I am grateful to all of you: Darci A. Bible, Summit County ESC; Diane R. Borden, Southwestern School District; Kelly Dailey, Southwestern School District; Mary Ann Falligant, ACT Houston; Tia M. Howe, Yarmouth School Department; Maria Rella, Boise School District; and Leon Smith, Sr., El Paso Independent School District.

My final thank you is to all of the teachers and students who added the spice and flavor to this book with your anecdotes and advice. The following teachers, administrators, substitute teachers, and students have given freely of their advice.

Teachers, Administrators, Substitute Teachers, and Others

Gabe Aguilar
Diane Amendt
Barbara Arient
Austin Independent
  School District
Dottie Bailey
Sarah Barten
Shirley Byassee
Jan Christian
Dion Clark
Shirley Clark
Dr. Arturo Delgado, Supt.
  SBCUSD
Nancy DeMaggio
David Emrick
Linda Evans
Sidney Gaskins
Helena Vendrzyk Gordon
Phyllis Guy
Kristin Hilsabeck

Elizabeth Hodgson
Susan Johnson
Cindy Martin
Ken Martinez, Principal
Rachel Vogelpohl Meyen
Linda Meyer
Marsha Moyer
Dr. Virginia Newlin,
  Principal
Joe Nutt
Bob Ostrander
Michael Peterson
Miccilina Piraino
Betty Rosentrater
Lori Rozelle
San Bernardino City Unified
  School District
Anne Sandel
Eric Sheninger, Principal
Joan Smith

JP Stein

Sally Steinbrunn

Brandi Stephens

Jane Stewart

Sandra Stiles

Dr. Harold Vollkommer

Richard Weber, Principal

Beth Ann Willstrop

Renee Zerbel

Delaine Zody

Students

Michael E.

Ruby P.

Drew K.

Jack S.

Andrew S.

Elfrieda

Natalie G.

Walker P.

BRIEF CONTENTS

CONTENTS

CHAPTER 1

An Introduction to Substitute Teaching

Effectiveness Essentials

- Substitute teachers serve an important role in the school setting.

- Schools cannot run without the services of substitute teachers.

- A variety of motivations drive the desire to substitute teach.

- Student perceptions of the substitute teacher's role provide useful information.

- The requirements for and training of substitute teachers vary from state to state.

The substitute teacher is a valued member of a classroom team, a pinch hitter in emergencies. The brave substitute may be unfamiliar with the school, the class, the grade level, the materials, and the content. In addition to all the ambiguity that goes along with the position, 30-plus students sometimes mistake the arrival of a substitute for party time. I have seen students who wear angel wings and halos with their own teachers suddenly demoralize substitutes.

The Purpose of This Book

The purpose of this book is to make sure that you are as prepared as you can be before assuming the role of substitute teacher and to address your concerns about the tough and scary stuff, especially the lack of adequate preparation for the job. You may be a very competent person with a great deal of life experience, but if you haven't been a teacher or are not currently enrolled in a teacher preparation program, you cannot assume that substitute teaching will come naturally to you. Some job training in advance will help you enjoy the "good stuff" sooner and ameliorate the "tough and scary" stuff as much as possible.

The Substitute Teacher's Guide to Success will walk you step by step through the essential skills and strategies that will lead you to a dynamic and fulfilling experience in the world of substitute teaching. You will learn how to apply for a job; what your teacher expects from you; what to do when kids tell you, "That's not how our teacher does it"; and how to initiate your own routines, manage the classroom, discipline when needed, begin and end the day, and provide productive activities in between. There are many shortcuts you can take and these will be addressed in concluding chapters with resources, Web sites, and lesson planning sites.

The guide is geared to the requirements of the No Child Left Behind Act, which mandates the use of research-based strategies to teach standards-based lessons. No longer must substitute teachers rely only on the proverbial "bag of tricks." While you will want to have some backup if the teacher leaves no lesson plans, this guide will provide you with backup that is in accordance with NCLB mandates.

As you read the Contents, choose those chapters that meet your immediate needs. You need not read the chapters in order. Now relax and strap yourself in for an exhilarating ride as you prepare for substitute teaching.

What Is a Substitute Teacher?

Students have their own ideas about the role and job description for the substitute teacher, and throughout the book you will read students' perceptions of substitutes. It is apparent from the definitions that follow that the younger the child, the more positive the view of subs. They are seen as helpers in the elementary grades, but by high school, some students have a more cynical perspective. It is useful to hear from students, however limited their experience with subs may be.

Schools cannot run without substitute teachers. There are many reasons that subs are needed. Teachers get sick, take maternity leave, or need time off to care for sick kids and parents. Teachers are required to attend inservice sessions or workshops and conferences, or to mentor beginning teachers in their own classrooms. Teachers also take personal "mental health" days, requiring the services of a substitute.

In response to the question, "What is a substitute teacher?"

It's a teacher that comes when the real teacher isn't there.

Ruby, age 6
Kindergarten

When a substitute comes to our class we behave better because we want our sub to give us a good report to our real teacher.

Drew, age 7
Second grade

When a substitute teacher comes to our class everyone gets a little too excited and starts correcting him or her on everything she says. A substitute teacher is someone who takes place of the teacher when he's out to lunch or something. A substitute teacher differs from the real teacher because substitute teachers don't know what they're doing half of the time. Subs should always remember that they are the bosses and that they never have to be afraid to use the good cop bad cop routine.

Jack, age 10
Fifth grade

A substitute teacher is someone who fills in for your regular teacher when she has something to do. It is usually someone you do not know. You might have a "school sub," which is a person who only subs at your school and is your usual sub. You might not have one, so you will just have a lot of random subs.

Andrew, age 11
Sixth grade

A teacher other than your own who fills in for your everyday teacher when they are gone. They don't teach every day and get paid less. Usually they also get less respect.

Michael, age 12
Seventh grade

A substitute teacher is an extra teacher sent in when the other original teacher is sick or can't teach the class. Sometimes the students refer to subs as doormats because most let you walk all over them.

Elfrieda, age 18
Continuation high school

Why Substitute Teach?

Many teachers I know across the country started out as subs prior to or while earning their credentials. Probably the best reason to become a substitute teacher is to find out if you really want to teach. It is rare in other professions to have opportunities to "try out" the job on a part-time basis. You can learn a great deal about how to set up a classroom environment, how to write effective lesson plans, how to establish routines, and how to use various discipline and management strategies. You will be better prepared than most students should you choose to enter a credential program later on. Here are some teachers who chose the sub route prior to earning a full credential.

Voices of Teachers and Subs

Substitute Speaks...

I became a substitute teacher because I wanted to work part-time while my children were in school. I have also thought I might like to get my credential when my kids are a little older and thought I should see if I like teaching. That was six years ago. I guess I like it.

Jane Stewart
Credential candidate

Teacher Talks...

I first became a sub because I was in grad school working on a degree in sociology and had flexibility with the job, choosing what days I could work. I also enjoyed working with kids so it seemed like an easy way to earn money. I immediately fell in love with teaching and felt like I had a natural "knack" for it. The students responded well in all of the classes that I taught in and I was asked to fill in for several long-term positions. I found my calling quite by accident!

Barbara Arient
High school special education

Retired Teacher Speaks...

The rewards for subbing are many. An aspiring teacher who is waiting to be hired permanently can experience many different classroom teachers' styles and methods. The substitute might want to take a notebook to sketch bulletin boards or write down management/discipline plans. Substitutes may also have a chance to try out different age groups and gain a great deal of experience adjusting to the different classes.

Joan Smith
Reading specialist

Teacher Talks...

I became a sub so that I could acquire some experience, hone my craft, and hopefully, make a positive name for myself in the school district. Oh, and I needed the minute amount of cash, as well.

David Emrick
Fifth grade teacher

Some retired teachers go back to subbing because they miss the stimulation teaching provides and, most important, they miss working with the students. Other subs I know miss the camaraderie of the school environment and miss friends who are still teaching full time.

Retired Teacher/Substitute Speaks...

I was retired from teaching for one year. I missed the camaraderie of my fellow teachers but most of all I missed the kids. I decided to substitute but only at my former school. I had always taught sixth grade and was reluctant to sub for all the grade levels, especially the primary grades. Much to my surprise, I found I enjoyed teaching different grade-level classes, even the primary grades. Each age has something special about it. Although I know I wouldn't enjoy, say, being in first grade all year, it's been fun to "mix it up." Also, since I've been doing this now for two years, most of the students at the school know me. It feels great being somewhere where "everyone knows your name" (my apologies to Cheers). I've found that each grade level has its pros and cons but, since I'm in each class for such a short span of time, I can just enjoy the pros and tolerate the cons.

Sally Steinbrunn

Varieties of Subbing Situations

There are many kinds of subs, many different reasons for subbing, and variations in experience and qualifications. Some subs want long-term assignments so they can get to know a class of students for more than a day at a time. Some long-term subs remain in the same class for weeks or months, often because of maternity leave but also because of illness, family obligations, and other emergency situations. Others are happy with the day-to-day sub experience, which carries less responsibility for long-term planning, instruction, assessment, and test preparation, to name a few of the roles the "regular" teacher plays.

Some subs prefer one-school assignments where they know the students and the other teachers. This is a very stress-free solution for teachers who have retired from the school or parents who have their own children enrolled there. Subs attached to one school are familiar with the community, know many of the teachers and students, and know the policies and procedures cold.

Many subs are experienced teachers who take time off to raise children and for a multitude of reasons want to maintain a connection with students. Subbing provides decent pay to augment household income, some benefits,

Substitute Speaks...

My wife and I are both substitute teachers, she in elementary only and I in elementary, middle, and high schools, although I probably will not continue in high schools beginning in the fall. We substitute in about seven different elementary schools, and I substitute in two different middle schools and have substituted in two different high schools. We've been at it since the spring semester of 2005 (I actually began in December of 2004 in kindergarten, my first ever substitute experience). My wife and I moved to our current home (Mebane, NC) from the concrete, steel, and glass jungle of Cary, NC, in November of 2004. After graduation from college was assured for our four children, and their marriages behind us, we left the work scene and decided to move and downsize since it would be just the two of us. We now live on a lake across from Eastern Alamance High School and Woodlawn Middle School. Since we were too young to totally retire, we decided to become substitute teachers. My wife was a certified schoolteacher (South Carolina), but over the course of our nomadic lifestyle of 29 years in the Air Force, she only taught after our four were in school and only at the preschool level. I, on the other hand, had no experience in teaching except for instructor duties (I was a pilot) in the Air Force and at my three-year final assignment, commander of the Air Force ROTC organization at NC State University. It truly has been a baptism of fire for both of us to begin substituting as schoolteachers, especially since most of the schools we sub in are Title I schools. Even though we've been in the teaching environment only a short time (2 $\frac{1}{2}$ years), we've seen a lot.

Bob Ostrander

built-in variety, and, most important for some potential subs, flexibility. Experienced subs can choose the days they work and even choose schools and/or grade levels.

Some districts may ask that you sub where needed each and every day. That can be stressful yet fun for those subs who like the variety of different

Teacher/Substitute Speaks...

No lesson plans, no grading, no parent conferences, need I say more? The fact that I am a mother of four children in middle and elementary schools, I find it to be convenient to work when and if I want.

Linda Evans
Credentialed teacher and sub

schools and grade levels. Once you are known at a school, teachers may request you, and then you may just find yourself busy enough to call one school site your home away from home.

The Ups and Downs of Subbing

Every position, profession, or job has the good stuff, the tough stuff, and even the scary stuff. Subbing is no different. Following is a summary to help you decide if the good stuff outweighs the tough stuff and scary stuff.

The Good Stuff

- Opportunity to make long-range career decision
- Preparation for teaching if you have already made your decision
- Ability to pick up great ideas for instruction, room arrangement, and so on
- As a day-to-day sub, freedom from meetings, long-range planning, grading, reporting, and conferencing with parents
- Meeting new people
- Fun, flexibility, and variety
- Freedom from "teacher homework" when the final bell sounds

The Tough Stuff

- Vague or missing lesson plans
- Less pay per diem than a regular teacher
- No benefits except in rare districts where you are long-term subbing
- Diverse students with differing needs, interests, and abilities
- Changing schools, classes, or grade levels on little notice every day you sub

The Scary Stuff

- Undisciplined students
- Student perceptions that sub time is "party" time
- Little authority and no leverage with grades
- Only on-the-job training, no formal teacher preparation

The Importance of Training for Substitute Teachers

Our representatives in Congress understand the need for prior training of substitute teachers. In researching the proposed Substitute Teaching Act, HR 3345, the House of Representatives has found that as much as one full year of a child's elementary and secondary education is taught by substitute teachers. On any given day in the United States, substitute teachers teach more than 270,000 classes.

Parents should be very concerned about this statistic, and, therefore, the House of Representatives is trying to mandate training for subs. According to the findings, formal training of substitute teachers has been shown to improve the quality of education, lower school district liability, reduce the number of student and faculty complaints, and increase retention rates of substitute teachers. Other findings from the House of Representatives that are fueling the need for substitute teacher training are outlined in the Statistics boxed feature.

Statistics

- Fewer than one in four school districts provides training for substitute teachers.
- No training is given to substitute teachers in 77% of school districts in the United States.
- More than half (56%) of school districts never have a face-to-face interview with substitute teaching candidates.
- Poorly trained substitute teachers have a negative impact on student academic performance and achievement.
- Schools with high concentrations of disadvantaged populations are more likely to be taught by less qualified permanent teachers and underprepared substitute teachers.
- Nine out of the 10 lowest-ranked states in the National Assessment of Educational Progress (NAEP) testing allowed substitute teachers with only a high school diploma to teach in their schools.
- In 28 states, principals may hire anyone with a high school diploma or a general equivalency diploma (GED) who is age 18 or older.
- Schools with lower academic achievement are twice as likely to allow less qualified substitutes in the classroom.

Source: http://thomas.loc.gov/cgi-bin/query/z?c110:H.R.3345.

Retired Teacher/Substitute Speaks...

Subbing isn't for the faint-hearted. Subbing is for teachers who can bring skills, patience, experience, inspiration, and empathy to a classroom of people with potential. Pitfalls and possibilities abound. To make a day of subbing worthwhile for the students, supportive of the regular teacher, and satisfying for the sub requires preparation. It also requires flexibility, creativity, and a sense of humor.

Betty Rosentrater

Betty retired after more than 30 years teaching K–12 in the U.S. and at International Schools in Nicaragua, Honduras, Mexico, and Cameroon. Now 82, she finds she still loves to learn and to teach.

The following article appeared in *Education Week* in September 2007. It addresses the need to effectively train substitute teachers. Some districts tend to staff classrooms with uncertified substitute teachers who have very minimal qualifications. Given that the majority of states don't require substitute teachers to have more than a high school diploma, and the fact that way too many classrooms are staffed by subs, this analysis presents a compelling argument for providing effective training of substitute teachers and reducing the need for so many subs, especially in high-poverty areas.

A Journalist Reports...

Policies Allow Districts to Cut Corners with Substitutes

Vaishali Honawar

Thousands of students in districts struggling to find teachers entered classrooms in the past few weeks staffed by substitutes. But the bar that Congress and most states and school systems have set for such educators is much lower than for regular classroom teachers.

The majority of states don't require substitutes to have more than a high school diploma. Nor do they require districts to give them any training before they set foot in classrooms.

In Prince George's County, Md., administrators had to rope in 140 subs for the opening day of classes after the 134,000-student district, located just outside Washington, failed to fill more than 10 percent of vacancies.

The figure, while high, is by no means unusual. Most big-city districts draw from large pools of substitutes to make up for teacher absenteeism and vacancies throughout the school year. The Substitute Teaching Institute at Utah State University in Logan, Utah, which helps districts develop training programs, estimates that 8 to 10 percent of teachers in classrooms on any given day, or 274,000 teachers, are substitutes.

Despite subs' rampant use, the issue has failed until recently to capture the attention of federal lawmakers as they discuss reauthorization of the No Child Left Behind Act. At present, the law only "strongly" recommends that long-term substitute teachers meet requirements for being "highly qualified"; it does nothing more to address minimum qualifications for those teachers. A House draft for the reauthorization proposes grants to high-poverty districts to provide training for substitutes.

The $5\frac{1}{2}$-year-old law does require that parents of children in a Title I school be notified if their children have been taught for four weeks or more by a teacher who is not highly qualified. The law leaves it up to

(*continued*)

(*Continued*)

states and districts to define "long-term substitute" ("Draft NCLB Bill Intensifies the Discussion," Sept. 5, 2007).

Jack Jennings, the president of the Center on Education Policy, a research and advocacy organization in Washington, said the need for subs appears to be rising as a large number of teachers from the baby boom generation retire and districts labor to fill jobs. "There has been a lack of publicity on the issue [of substitute-teacher qualifications]. Policymakers deal with issues brought to their attention," said Mr. Jennings, a former aide to House Democrats. "Otherwise, it just slips by and is not addressed."

No College Necessary

Parental notification—the federal government's only requirement of Title I schools that use long-term substitutes—is better than nothing but hasn't been very effective, observers say.

While working on a report covering some Southern states in 2003, Barnett Berry, the president of the Center for Teaching Quality, a teacher-advocacy and -research group in Hillsborough, N.C., said his group found that superintendents in some rural areas who were having a hard time finding teachers would move substitutes from school to school to circumvent the requirement.

"It is a loophole that has been used by superintendents, and quite frankly, I don't believe that this is necessarily a malintention," Mr. Berry said.

Geoffrey Smith, the president of the Substitute Teaching Institute, said most districts consider 21 school days or more to be long-term subbing.

At present, 28 states require nothing more than a high school diploma for subs, even long-term ones, although Mr. Smith pointed out that only about 10 percent of those in the current workforce hold that minimal qualification.

About a third are certified, and another third hold at least a bachelor's degree, he added. Still, 90 percent of the substitutes don't receive any formal training before taking charge of a classroom. "That's a big area that needs to be addressed and worked on," Mr. Smith said. A handful of states have, in recent years, taken steps to improve the quality of their substitute-teacher workforce. For instance, California, which requires all substitutes to have at least a bachelor's degree, also demands that its long-term substitutes go through a teacher-credentialing program at a college or university. Florida, too, puts substitutes through a training program that has proved effective at preparing candidates for schools, according to Mr. Smith.

In the 57,000-student Boston district, substitutes take an online test before they are granted a job interview. They must have at least a bachelor's degree, and undergo a training program designed for the district by the Substitute Teaching Institute.

Some districts that do not set a high bar on formal education and training qualifications still say they seek out the most qualified candidates. In Austin, Texas, the 81,450-student district has 1,700 substitutes on its rolls at all times, said Kristen Hilsabeck, the substitute-services coordinator. Although subs don't have to have a bachelor's degree, about 75 percent do, she said, and 30 percent are certified.

Ms. Hilsabeck said the district also gives first preference to those who are highly qualified in the subjects they are expected to teach, when administrators first try to fill a position.

In Maryland's Prince George's County schools, about 75 percent of substitute teachers are certified or have at least a bachelor's degree, said Randy Thornton, the director of human resources for the district.

In an interview, Mr. Thornton said the district still had 110 vacancies that were being filled by substitutes. However, he added, his office was working "round the clock" to recruit teachers.

The county considers a substitute who teaches for 15 consecutive days to be long-term. Mr. Thornton could not say how many of the vacancies were in Title I schools—those receiving federal aid for disadvantaged students under that part of the NCLB law—and thus could trigger the parental-notification clause.

What's "Highly Qualified"?
A big area of concern for teacher advocates is that many substitutes—and particularly the least qualified—end up in high-poverty schools.

"In well-heeled communities, you will find substitute teachers who are certified, who want to be a teacher there, and will substitute for several years to get into the good graces of administrators," said Mr. Berry of the Center for Teaching Quality. "In rural and high-needs urban communities, what you find are people off the street, people who are willing to work for $10 an hour."

What further complicates the situation of finding and setting a bar for substitute teachers is the concern some observers, such as Mr. Berry, feel over the current definition of "highly qualified" under the NCLB law, which, they believe, is inadequate.

Under current guidelines, a highly qualified teacher must have a bachelor's degree, hold full state certification, and demonstrate competence in the subject he or she teaches. "I refuse the claim that highly

(*continued*)

(Continued)

qualified teachers are really highly qualified," Mr. Berry said. "It is nothing more than a minimal qualification.

"Substitute teachers ought to be teachers who know the curriculum, know the program, know the kids," he added.

Yet others say that rather than focus on the qualifications for substitutes, they would prefer it if the law ensured that fewer students were taught by substitutes.

"Districts need to look at teacher absences . . . and focus on it," said Ross Wiener, the policy director for the Education Trust, a Washington-based group that promotes educational improvement for poor and minority children. "They ought to be looking at their absence policy, . . . attrition rates, and see what they can do to stabilize staff," he added.

Mr. Jennings of the Center on Education Policy said lawmakers need to approach the issue of improving substitute-teacher quality in a "commonsensical" manner.

"There should be at least an investigation of this issue as a problem," he said. "We need to look at how many substitute teachers are there, how long they stay in schools, and are they on the way to fulfilling requirements for certification."

Source: As first appeared in *Education Week,* September 12, 2007. Reprinted with permission from Editorial Projects in Education.

In light of the need for better training for substitute teachers, as you prepare to secure and submit an application to your preferred district(s), a good question to ask is, "Where can I find opportunities to learn more about subbing?" You may discover that your local college or university offers courses in subbing, or your local districts may offer substitute teaching orientations. Many Web sites listed in Chapter 15 will lead you to very useful information. Now it is time to consider applying for a substitute teaching position. Read on.

CHAPTER 2

Applying for a Position

There are some convenient ways to apply to be a substitute teacher. First, check to see if your selected district(s) has a Web site where application materials are available. Many sites have online application procedures that even make the seemingly repetitive process enjoyable. If the application cannot be downloaded or completed online, you may need to visit the district office in person, or you can request application materials by phone.

There are several steps you can take in applying for a position as a substitute teacher. Whether you are a retired or a fully credentialed teacher or not, when you apply to a new district you will have to follow most of the steps outlined below.

Identify Preferred Districts

1. The first step in applying for a position is to identify the districts you are prepared to work for. You may want to check with a few districts in your locale because some districts may have greater needs than others. The requirements will differ from district to district, and they have their own application forms and processes. You can either call or check online by entering the term *substitute teacher application* along with the *district name*. You may want to personally visit the district office to get your application materials.

Determine Whether You Meet the Qualifications

2. The second step directly influences your choice of districts. Many districts require a bachelor's degree at minimum, while some will let you skate by with less than that. In fact, a majority of states (28) will let you sub with just a high school diploma. The application will alert you to other requirements that you may need to meet.

Fill Out an Application

3. Obtain and fill out an application. You need to have all your documentation available to make the task easier. Applications differ from district to district, but essentially the information required is the same. All applications for substitute teaching include the following elements, although some districts go beyond the basics. You will need to provide personal contact information, educational and work history, transcripts, licenses, background checks, fingerprinting, references, and taxpayer identification. Some applications, like this one from the Austin Independent School District, can be downloaded from the Web.

AUSTIN INDEPENDENT SCHOOL DISTRICT
APPLICATION FOR SUBSTITUTE SERVICES

Office of Human Resources/Substitute Office

AN EQUAL OPPORTUNITY EMPLOYER
1111 W. 6TH Street, Building D-130
Austin, Texas 78703-5338
Telephone: (512) 414-2611

FOR OFFICE USE
DATE ————————————
Degree Code ————————
SSF Results ————————
DPS sent ——————————
DPS rec. ——————————
Approval sent ———————
Received ——————————
Orient. Ltr. ————————
Orientation ————————

Profile

SubPay ——————————

I-9   W-4

POSITION(S) APPLYING FOR (Circle Preference):

1. Substitute Teacher   2. Classified / Clerical Substitute (Teacher Assistant, Security Guard, Clerk, Secretary, etc.)

Are you CURRENTLY a student teacher?   ❑ YES   ❑ NO   UNIVERSITY_____

PERSONAL INFORMATION

Last Name: _____   First Name: _____

Middle: _____   Social Security Number: _____

Other names which may appear on official records: _____

Present Street Address: Street _____

City, State _____   Zip _____

(Area Code) Telephone Number _____   Alternate Telephone Number _____

Are you prevented from lawfully becoming employed in this country because of visa or immigration status?   ❑ Yes   ❑ No   If yes, please explain:
_____

Are you fluent in a language other than English?   ❑ Yes   ❑ No   If yes, please list:
_____

Have you ever been employed by the Austin I.S.D.?   ❑ Yes   ❑ No

If yes, position held: _____   Name of supervisor: _____

Dates of employment: _____   Reason for leaving: _____

School/Department: _____   Name at time of employment: _____

(continued)

Are you retired with the Texas Retirement System (TRS)?   ❑ Yes   ❑ No

If yes, date of retirement: _____

What Texas school district are you retired from: _____

Do you have relatives who are either a member of the Board of Trustees of the Austin Independent School District or who are employed in any capacity in the Austin Independent School District?   ❑ Yes   ❑ No

If yes, please list all: _____

_____

EDUCATION

Name of Institution _____   Location _____

Date of Graduation _____   Level of Degree (BA, MA, Ph.D) or no. of college hours if no degree _____

   Major, Minor _____

   High School _____

   Colleges _____

   Other _____

TEACHING CERTIFICATES/ENDORSEMENTS/LICENSES

Type of Certificate/Endorsement/License (State, Date of Expiration) _____

Subjects/Grades/Areas Covered _____

TEACHING EXPERIENCE (include student teaching)

From: _____ Mo./Year   To: _____ Mo./Year

Name and Address of School Principal; Grade or Subject Taught _____

_____

How many total years of teaching experience do you have? _____

OTHER WORK EXPERIENCE

From: _____ Mo./Year   To: _____ Mo./Year

Name of Employer; Address _____

Kind of Work _____

CRIMINAL HISTORY

Have you ever been convicted of a felony or misdemeanor?   ❑ Yes   ❑ No

If yes, please explain in the space below: (NOTE: Conviction of a crime is not necessarily a bar to employment):

Offense: _____   Date Convicted: _____

Disposition: _____   Comments: _____

REFERENCES

Do not use relatives

Full Name and Title of Reference _____

(Area Code) Telephone Number _____

In case of emergency, please contact   Name _____

Telephone Number _____

I certify that all the information contained in this application (and accompanying resume, if any) is true and correct, and further understand that any misstatement or omission of information is grounds for rejection of employment, or if employed, termination from the Austin Independent School District (AISD). I authorize all persons listed to give the District any and all information regarding my previous employment and education and any other pertinent information they may have, personal or otherwise, and release all parties, such persons, and the District from liability for any damage that may result from furnishing same to the District. In addition, I authorize AISD to obtain copies of any information pertaining to any criminal history record maintained by any law enforcement agency and to use said information for the purpose of evaluating my application for employment. Furthermore, it is understood that this application becomes the property of AISD, which reserves the right to accept or reject it.

Date _____   Signature _____

"Criminal History Record Information Authorization" Form and proof of college (to be a substitute teacher) must be submitted with this application.

WE DO NOT ACCEPT FAXED DOCUMENTS

Permission to reproduce this application comes from Kristen Hilsabeck, the substitute-services coordinator.

From the San Bernardino City Unified School District comes the requirement for a basic skills test (California Basic Educational Skills Test) in addition to all the other similarly requested information. The application is appended to the following letter from the Assistant Superintendent for Human Resources, Dr. Harold Vollkommer, and is reprinted with permission from Dr. Arturo Delgado, Superintendent of the San Bernardino City Unified School District.

Note that references are required by all of the districts I contacted. Also required are criminal record checks done at your own expense from fingerprints. Contact your local police department or university campus police. Some districts require a written statement from the applicant and an interview as well. You can anticipate interview questions such as: Why do you want to sub? Why this district? What grades or subjects do you feel qualified for? What skills do you bring to a subbing position? What experience do you have teaching in schools or other institutions? What do you see as the challenges of substitute teaching? What will you do if the teacher has not left adequate plans? What is your philosophy of discipline as a substitute teacher?

Arturo Delgado, Ed.D.
Superintendent
Harold J. Vollkommer, Ed.D.
Assistant Superintendent

Dear Applicant:

We are pleased that you are interested in substitute teaching with the San Bernardino City Unified School District. Substitute teachers play a vital role in the daily operation of our schools. No matter if it is a day, a week or a month, substitute teachers make significant contributions to the education of our students.

Please complete and return the enclosed application form and required materials. Prior to being considered for an interview, it is important that you provide our office with the following:

Completed substitute application form
Copy of document indicating you have passed the CBEST
Copies of all credentials (if applicable)
Copy of university transcripts with posted bachelor's degree

If you are hired as a substitute teacher, you will need to provide our office with official transcripts, original social security card, original CBEST documentation and tuberculosis clearance. In addition, San Bernardino City Unified School District requires that all employees pass a drug screening and fingerprinting clearance prior to employment.

Thank you for considering the San Bernardino City Unified School District. If I can be of any assistance to you, please do not hesitate to call our office at (909) 381-1115.

Sincerely,
Harold Vollkommer
HAROLD VOLLKOMMER
Assistant Superintendent
Certificated Human Resources
HUMAN RESOURCES DIVISION
777 North F Street • San Bernardino, CA 92410 • (909) 381-1228 • Fax (909) 884-9830

San Bernardino City Unified School District   Date _____
          Human Resources Division
777 North F Street, San Bernardino, CA 92410   Soc. Sec. No.: _____
          Telephone: (909) 381-1115

CERTIFICATED APPLICATION FORM
An Equal Opportunity/ADA/504/Title IX/ADEA Employer

Position for which you are applying: <u>SUBSTITUTE TEACHER</u>

Name _____
          Last   **First**   **Middle**
Present Address: _____
                                              Number & Street

_____   _____
   City   State   Zip Code   Home Telephone

                                                        _____
                                                                Cell Telephone

E-Mail Address: _____

Permanent Address: _____

Number & Street

_____   _____

| City | State | Zip Code | Telephone |

If there is someone who will know of your whereabouts at all times, please indicate:

_____   _____

| Name | Address | Telephone |

CERTIFICATION   Valid credential(s) held: (List specific title and expiration dates)

Type:_____   Expires:_____

Type:_____   Expires:_____

If you are in the process of applying for a California credential, list type and date of application:

Type:_____   Date:_____

Through which college or district? _____

List any foreign language you speak fluently: _____

Have you passed CBEST examination?   Yes_____   No_____

Are you NCLB compliant?   Yes_____   No_____   By what means?_____

Have you passed a subject matter examination (CSET, MSAT, Praxis, or NTE)?   Yes_____   No_____

If yes, in what subject?_____ Please include documentation.

HR-179 (Rev. 04/08)

TEACHING EXPERIENCE   Record all teaching experience in chronological order, last position first.
(Please include substitute teaching)

City or Town	State	Zip	Name of School	Grade/Subject Taught	Date From (Mo.,Yr.) To (Mo., Yr.)

STUDENT TEACHING EXPERIENCE

City or Town	State	Zip	Name of School	Grade/Subject Taught	Master Teacher	Dates From (Mo.,Yr.) To (Mo., Yr.)

(continued)

OTHER WORK EXPERIENCE (Including nonteaching work experience)

Name of Employer	Address·	Type of Employment	Dates of Employment From	To

PROFESSIONAL TRAINING

EDUCATION: College and/or University Training

	College/University & Location	Dates	Degree/Credential	Major	Minor
Undergraduate					
Graduate					

PERSONAL REFERENCES

It is necessary for us to have names, addresses, and phone numbers of at least three references who are acquainted with you and your work experience and/or education. **INCLUDE YOUR LAST EMPLOYER.**

Name of	Official Position	Address	Phone Number

OTHER MISCELLANEOUS INFORMATION

Have you ever been convicted of an offense other than a minor traffic violation? Yes_____ No_____
If so, please state the nature of the offense(s), date(s), city and state, and disposition on a separate sheet of paper. A conviction record is not an automatic bar to employment and the nature, recency, and disposition of an offense will be considered only as it relates to the job for which you are applying.

Have you ever been discharged or forced to resign from any position because of misconduct or unsatisfactory service?

Yes _____   No _____

If yes, attach a separate sheet stating circumstances, including dates, names, address of employers and causes.

Can you perform all job¬related functions of this position?

Yes _____   No _____   Comment _____

_____

_____

AGENCY FEE

The District has an agency-fee agreement with the Communication Workers of America (CWA). Every employee in the collective bargaining unit represented by the CWA must pay an agency fee to the Union within thirty days of commencement of assigned duties and each pay period thereafter for which compensation is received. For more explicit information regarding the agency fee, contact:

Communication Workers of America Local 9588
190 West G Street
Colton, CA 92324

Telephone (909) 422-8960

I hereby certify that all statements made hereon are true and correct to the best of my knowledge and authorize investigations of all statements herein recorded. I release from all liability persons and organizations reporting information required by this application.

_____   _____
        Date   Signature of Applicant

The San Bernardino City Unified School District does not discriminate on the basis of race, color, national origin, ancestry, ethnic group identification, religious creed, marital status, sex (including sexual harassment), sexual orientation, gender (identity or expression), disability (physical or mental) or age in any of its policies, procedures, or practices in compliance with the Title VI and Title VII of the Civil Rights Act of 1964 (pertaining to race, color, religion, sex and national origin); Title IX of the Education Amendments of 1972 (pertaining to gender); Section 504 of the Rehabilitation Act of 1973 (pertaining to disability); and Age Discrimination in the Employment Act of 1975 (pertaining to age 40 and over), the Americans with Disabilities Act of 1990, the federal Family and Medical Leave Act, the California Family Rights Act and the Fair Employment and Housing Act. This nondiscrimination policy covers admission, participation, and accessibility to any program or activity of the district and selection, advancement, discharge and other terms, conditions and privileges of employment. Inquiries regarding the equal opportunity policies, equal program accessibility policies and the filing of complaint procedures alleging discrimination, including sexual harassment, may be directed to the school principal/site administrator or to the District's Affirmative Action Director, 777 North F Street, San Bernardino, CA, (909) 381–1122.

SAN BERNARDINO CITY UNIFIED SCHOOL DISTRICT
Certificated Human Resources
777 North "F" Street
San Bernardino, CA 92410

TO: San Bernardino City Unified School District Applicant

This information shall be used only for research and statistical purposes relative to the District's employment practices and will in no way affect the individual's employment.

(continued)

HAROLD J. VOLLKOMMER
Assistant Superintendent
Human Resources Division

APPLICANT'S NAME: _____   Date: _____

Position applied for: _____

How did you find out about this vacancy: Magazine (specify) _____

Job Fair (specify) _____

Newspaper (specify) _____

Internet (specify) _____

Other: _____

Age Group: ❑ Under 40   ❑ 40 or over

Gender: ❑ F   ❑ M

Ethnic Category (check one):

❑ 100 American Indian or Alaska Native   ❑ 300 Native Hawaiian/Other Pacific Isl

❑ 200 Asian   ❑ 301 Hawaiian

❑ 201 Chinese   ❑ 302 Guamanian

❑ 202 Japanese   ❑ 303 Samoan

❑ 203 Korean   ❑ 304 Tahitian

❑ 204 Vietnamese   ❑ 399 Other Pacific Islander

❑ 205 Asian Indian   ❑ 400 Filipino

❑ 206 Laotian   ❑ 500 Hispanic or Latino

❑ 207 Cambodian   ❑ 600 Black/African American (not Hispanic)

❑ 208 Other Asian   ❑ 700 White (not Hispanic)

HR-43 (Rev. 12/06)

AUTHORIZATION TO RELEASE INFORMATION

As an applicant for the position of _____ with the San Bernardino City Unified School District, I am required to furnish information for use in determining my qualifications. In this regard, I authorize release of any and all information that you may have concerning me, including, but not limited to, information of a confidential or privileged nature, or any data or materials which have been sealed or agreed to be withheld pursuant to any prior agreement or court proceeding involving disciplinary matters.

I understand that I will not receive and am not entitled to know the contents of confidential reports received, and I further understand that these reports are privileged.

I hereby release, discharge, exonerate the San Bernardino City Unified School District, their agents and representatives, and any person furnishing information from any and all liability of every nature and kind arising out of the furnishing information from any and all liability of every nature and kind arising out of the furnishing and inspection of such documents, records, and other information, and this release shall be binding on my legal representatives, heirs, and assigns.

A photocopy of this release is to be considered as valid as an original.

Signed: _____

Date: _____

Revised April 2008

_____

SAN BERNARDINO CITY UNIFIED SCHOOL DISTRICT
SmartFind Express

Substitute Teacher Form

NAME _____ TELEPHONE (____)_____

ADDRESS_____ EMAIL _____

CITY_____ STATE _____ ZIP_____

SSN_____

Identify the days of the week you are available to work. Mark your choices with an "X".

IF YOU ARE AVAILABLE ALL DAYS, CHECK HERE _____

(A.M.) MON____ TUES____ WED____ THURS____ FRI____

(P.M.) MON____ TUES____ WED____ THURS____ FRI____

Please choose types of locations. Mark your choices with an "X".

TYPE OF LOCATION

_____ 101000 Elementary Schools   _____ 104000 Special Education Classes

_____ 102000 Middle Schools   _____ 105000 Preschools

_____ 103000 High Schools   _____ 106000 Bilingual Elementary

Organize Your Documents

4. Start to collect the needed documentation even before you apply. Have transcripts sent to you, apply for a background check, alert your references and let them know they will be contacted. Make a list of your education- and non-education-related employment as well as your educational history. Some applications require a statement, and you might draft one whether it is called for or not in preparation for a phone or in-person interview. Make copies of your credentials and certificates. Keep all documents in order in a file so you can easily choose what is required by each district you apply to.

Obtain Information on Prerequisite Exams

5. Apply for and take any prerequisite tests. Many states or school districts require that subs take tests certifying that they have basic skills in reading, writing, and

Apply It!

Purchase a file folder with multiple compartments and start to collect your documents and lists by category:

Transcripts
Licenses, certificates
Reference letters or addresses
Test scores on basic educational tests required by some districts
Lists of work and educational experience

Apply It!

Prepare answers to these questions and draft a statement describing your strengths, skills, and preparation for subbing.

1. Why do you want to sub?
2. Why this district?
3. What grades or subjects do you feel qualified for?
4. What skills do you bring to a subbing position?
5. What experience do you have teaching in schools or other institutions?
6. What do you see as the challenges of substitute teaching?
7. What will you do if the teacher has not left adequate plans?
8. What is your philosophy of discipline as a substitute teacher?

math. This is true in the state of California where CBEST (California Basic Educational Skills Test) is a prerequisite, not only for teachers, but for subs as well. These tests are assumed to verify that you are capable of filling in for a teacher. Make sure that you obtain sample tests online or test review booklets and the testing schedule as some tests are given just a few times per year.

Identify Preferred Subjects and Grade Levels

6. Be prepared to identify what grades and subjects you are prepared to sub in. You may be asked for this information in the interview or on the application itself. Be honest in your replies as you do not want to be stuck in a home economics class if you can't boil an egg or trapped in a physics class when you barely passed the subject yourself. Kindergarten teachers and special education teachers require special skills and attitudes, so if you are not up to the task, be honest up front.

Familiarize Yourself with Calling Systems

7. Many school districts use an automated call system when a teacher is going to be absent instead of having the individual school secretary notify you. Become

familiar with the system your district uses and learn how you can log on to it. You stand a better chance of getting consistent work if you know how the automated system works.

Aesop is one such placement tool for K–12 school districts. Unlike traditional sub placement systems, Aesop completely automates the process of substitute placement and absence management for over 1,800 school districts worldwide. The system is efficient for district administrators, principals, and teachers who can make contact online or by phone anytime and anywhere. On Aesop subs can look for jobs and teachers who need subs can upload lesson plans. The Web site is www.frontlineplacement.com/ education.

Subfinder is another site that districts use to find substitutes and vice versa. After the system receives a call reporting absences, Subfinder begins searching for qualified substitutes. The Web site is www.crsadvancedtechnology.com/ products/sub-finder.html#substitutes.

Another system, Callplus at www.subcaller.com, promises the same sort of automated service. There are many other automated systems in place. When you apply, ask which system, if any, the district uses. Some may even find subs the old-fashioned way by having the school secretary use a list to call subs on the actual day or day before the anticipated absence.

Make an Appearance

8. Make an effort to visit individual schools and introduce yourself to the school secretary and the administrators. Although districts, not individual schools, make the hiring decisions, you are more likely to be called as a sub if you have volunteered at the school, if your child attends the school, or if you just present yourself as a prepared professional who is greatly interested in the position. The more the school gets to know you, both before and after you land a job, the morc likely it is that you will land the long-term position in case of sudden illness, maternity leave, unanticipated leave of absence, or firing.

Submit the Application

9. Finally, you when you submit your application, make sure it is edited, complete, signed, and dated. Make a copy for your own records. Find out from the district when you can expect to hear from them. Think positively and begin to prepare for an interview. Equally important is preparing for your first substitute teaching assignment.

District Substitute Teacher Handbooks

Issues of due process, pay, automated sub finder systems, health benefits, responsibilities, and so on are often addressed in a district's substitute teacher's handbook, and you should ask if one exists even before you apply to the district. Some district handbooks can be located online. Beside the issues of pay, health benefits, and due process, you will find a wealth of information in these handbooks.

In the next chapter you will find samples of substitute teacher handbooks from actual schools that are even more specific. They are peculiar to the school site and you should collect one from each school site that provides one. Read on.

CHAPTER 3

Preparing for Your First Day of Subbing

Effectiveness Essentials

- Familiarize yourself with your district, school, and its community.

- Keep a calendar and maintain up-to-date contact information.

- Check out how you will be notified.

- Determine details of the assignment.

- Network with teachers and other subs for advice and information.

- Gather some basic supplies for subbing.

Even before you step into the classroom for the first time, there are steps you can take to ease the transition to your subbing assignments. Take the time to get to know your school and the surrounding community if you are unfamiliar with it. Many subs are one-school subs, especially those who have taught in the district or have children at a particular school. But if you are one of those subs just beginning a career and testing the waters, you will want to become familiar with the district and schools. You can prepare for assignments ahead of time by getting to know the school and surrounding community where you plan on subbing and by gathering some basic supplies in anticipation of your first assignment.

Orient Yourself to the District/Community/ School Site

You can use these suggestions for getting to know your school district, specific school, and the surrounding community. During interviews it is very important that you know about the school and community, and you can convey your interest by sharing some of your observations.

- *Attend a school board meeting.*   You can even introduce yourself informally to the board members as a new substitute teacher. They will be impressed that you took the time to attend.
- *Visit your school.*   Take some time to visit school sites, and if you choose to be a one- or two-school sub, this will enable you to find the school and see how long the commute takes. Try out your route to school during the times you will be traveling back and forth to see what traffic is like or how to time your arrival by rapid transit. In addition, visiting the site early will help you feel more comfortable in your new surroundings. Introduce yourself to the school secretary, who will most likely be your contact when your services are needed.
- *Get to know your community.*   Relocation to a new community may be the deciding factor in becoming a sub, either because you are retiring from teaching and moving to a more hospitable climate or moving with young children and want a part-time job. Settle down as soon as possible so you can get a feel for the community and its schools.
- *Surf the school and district Web sites.*   You will find a great deal of information here that you will need to know. Many schools have a Web site of their own and while you surf you can choose some schools that are in proximity to your home or apartment. Most important, you can learn a great deal about district and school policies and procedures. Every school has its own history and challenges. You'll be better equipped to follow policies and procedures correctly if you get the most information beforehand.
- *Read the community phone directory and local newspaper.*   You will glean a great deal of information about an unfamiliar community by reading these

sources of good information. Learn the history of the town and read the local newspaper to find out what the local issues are.

- *Check on how you will be notified of assignments.* It is very possible that your district will use an automated telephone/Internet service such as the one used in Orange County in Southern California, called SEMS (Substitute Employee Management System), www.ocde.us/sems.asp, or another system mentioned in Chapter 2. Even if you are not in Orange County, if you go to the site you will have a better idea of how these automated systems work. They result in higher sub position fill rates, because they let teachers notify the school earlier and eliminate the need for school secretaries to vie for, and schedule, substitutes at the school site.

- *Most important, check with the district to see if they provide a substitute teaching handbook.* On the Web I found many of these up-to-date, district-specific resources. While the guide you are reading will cover much of the same material and more, the district-specific handbooks are required reading for new substitute teachers.

Use the following list to ask the right questions if there is no substitute handbook for the district or the specific school site. These are all among the most important topics, and you want to be sure that you have the answers, especially if no handbook is provided.

Common Topics for Questions

- Responsibilities of the substitute teacher
- Automated sub calling instructions
- What to do upon arrival at the school site
- School and district discipline policy
- Students with special needs, including medication
- Responsibilities at the end of the day
- Handling injuries, accidents, and emergencies
- Pay and benefits

Ask About Necessary Forms Such As

- Substitute report
- Accident report form
- District calendar

You may find that, although the district has no generic substitute teacher handbook, many school administrators write their own. These are very specific to the school site. The first example of a school-specific, substitute teacher handbook comes from Eric Sheninger, principal of New Milford High School in New Jersey. As you peruse this very thorough handbook, you can imagine how much more confident a sub will feel after reading it. Notice that all key players are mentioned and policies and procedures are clearly delineated.

SCHOOL ARTIFACT

NEW MILFORD HIGH SCHOOL
TEACHER SUBSTITUTE HANDBOOK

September, 2008 NEW MILFORD HIGH SCHOOL
NEW MILFORD, NEW JERSEY

Dear Substitute Staff Member:

Welcome to New Milford High School. Thank you for your interest in serving on our substitute teaching staff. We hope that your experiences will be rewarding and you'll be encouraged to return. Whether you realize it or not, you are a bona fide staff member and assume regular teacher assignments.

This booklet is designed to provide you with a basic orientation to the school. It would be most desirable to have this information before coming on the job, as there is so much to remember in carrying out any daily assignment.

It is extremely important for substitutes to maintain the ongoing program in as normal a fashion as possible. We feel that if you know what is expected of you, our goal will be better achieved. In addition, you will experience a smooth day.

We appreciate your service in our school and thank you for helping make each day a productive one, educationally, for our students. Contact me or Mr. Manuppelli, Vice Principal, if we may be of assistance.

Very truly yours,
Eric Sheninger
Principal

TO: Substitute Teachers

FROM: Mr. Louis Manuppelli, Vice Principal

RE: *PROCEDURES*

- Attendance must be taken in *each class*. Please do not discharge students from subject class or study hall to any other part of the building to do assigned work. Students are to remain with you *in class for the entire period* and carry out the work which has been specified by the regular subject teacher.
- If you have a homeroom—please be sure any notes/slips included in homeroom folder are distributed to the students in the homeroom.
- Only ONE student is allowed out of the room with a pass at any one time. Any student leaving the classroom *must have a signed line in their planner (at rear of planner)*.
- Please record any student coming to class late without a pass and notify the Vice Principal's office at the end of the day.
- Absolutely NO iPods or cell phones are to be seen or used in class.

If you have questions, concerns, please see Mr. Manuppelli in the Main Office or call Mrs. Norton ext. 2000. Thank you!

Page 1

GENERAL DIRECTIONS

Report to the Main Office no later than 7:35 A.M.

Receive your packet of materials including attendance sheet, lesson plans, schedule for the day, bell schedule, and detailed instructions for carrying out specific responsibilities.

Report to the Department Chairperson for specific information that will help you in teaching the classes.

Follow the schedule given to you.

At the end of the day, report to the chairperson and leave plans plus a note to the absentee teacher indicating what was accomplished in the classes and any additional noteworthy observations.

Before you leave for the day, report to the Principal's secretary, Mrs. Gianfredi, and sign a voucher for the day.

CHAIRPERSONS:

LANGUAGE ARTS/WORLD LANGUAGE . . . . Mrs. DePoto

GUIDANCE. . . . . Mr. Carr

MATHEMATICS/BUSINESS . . . . Mrs. Miller

PHYSICAL EDUCATION/HEALTH/DRIVER
EDUCATION. . . . . Mr. Perrone

SCIENCE/FAMILY & CONSUMER
SCIENCE (Interim) . . . . Mrs. Catherine
Chin Quee-Smith

RELATED ARTS. . . . . Mr. Pevny
(Art/Industrial Arts/Music)

SOCIAL STUDIES/BUSINESS . . . . Mr. Wilson

Page 2

PARKING

Your actual parking space for each day will be issued through Mrs. Maria Esposito when she calls requesting your services for that day.

HOMEROOM—7:50–8:00 A.M.

NOTE: Homeroom will occur **PRIOR TO** Period 1. Students will be reporting directly to their homeroom at 7:50 A.M. (Classrooms are to be opened as early as possible—**7:45 A.M. at the latest**.)

■ Prepare for homeroom by getting attendance sheet ready (usually located in teacher mailbox if not included in substitute folder).

■ Take attendance and stand by with class for P. A. Flag salute and announcements done via P. A. Insist that students stand and **remain quiet** during flag salute.

■ Mark daily attendance sheet for those who are absent. Forward completed attendance roster to the Attendance Office immediately following homeroom (8:00 A.M.).

(continued)

(Continued)

- Distribute information to individual students or class in general (i.e. appointment slips, special bulletins, etc. that may be included in homeroom folder).
- Do not permit students out of the room without a written note from a staff member prior to the start of homeroom.

NOTE: Seniors are ineligible for the lounge during this time period.

- Make any announcements by other staff members as requested (example: assemblies, special bell schedules, etc.).
- Dismiss homeroom students to **first** period at 8:00 A.M.

Page 3

CLASSROOM DUTIES

- Report to assigned classes in time to receive students.
- Take attendance on separate attendance sheet and submit to Mrs. Schuette in the Attendance Office before the end of the period.
- Conduct a lesson for the class using plans received from the Mrs. Gianfredi, or the chairperson, or devise your own lesson in keeping with the work you have learned the class is covering. (Conduct the class with a minimum of disruption to the students' educational process.)
- If test or quiz is to be administered, establish proper test conditions and notify students of expectations. Circulate throughout the room so as to discourage cheating.
- Students may be excused *only* with written permission from a professional staff member which must be submitted **PRIOR** to start of class.
- Do not permit students to go elsewhere during class time. This includes use of phone, going to lounge, etc.
- Retain the students for the full time the class is scheduled for session.
- Lavatory excuses must be limited to one at a time.
- If you need help with reference to discipline problems:

  1. Send another student to see if the department chairperson is available to assist. If necessary, the chairperson can walk the student down to the Vice Principal's office. In the event the chairperson is not available, call a hall monitor or hall duty teacher and request that they walk the student to the Vice Principal's office. Be sure to have that person bring a note from you containing a short statement describing the disturbance.
  2. Follow-up on this case by seeing the department chairperson and/or the Vice Principal sometime later in the day.

- Collect and/or assign homework as directed by regular teacher.
- Be conscious of student safety at all times. If machinery and equipment are present in the room, only allow it to be used if you have prior permission of the department chairperson.

Page 4

HALL DUTY

- Pick up radio.
- Report to duty early, if possible, reporting to the area specified on your schedule.
- Basic responsibility is to supervise the students insuring that proper behavior and safety is maintained in the building.
- At the beginning of your duty, concentrate on clearing the lavatories of all students.
- Follow this by walking around the halls urging students to get to class.
- If two staff members are assigned, walk halls in *opposite directions*.
- During this portion of the period, continue to circulate, and when encountering a student in the hall, ask to see his/her hall pass (regular passes are signed by a teacher, with a date and time included).
- Students with valid passes are permitted to continue on their way.
- Students without valid passes are to be asked where they belong. If they belong in a class, study, etc. escort student to assigned room.
- Be aware that seniors are the only ones with independent studies. However, they are required to be somewhere in the building, *not* in the halls.
- Be sure to check all lavatories at least twice during the period.
- Report to the Vice Principal any student caught smoking or damaging the building.
- Visitors, who may be in the halls, must have passes from the Vice Principal, otherwise escort the visitors to the Main Office immediately.
- Seek the assistance of your hall duty partner if necessary—contact the Vice Principal by radio or ext. 2000 if serious problems are encountered.

Page 5

LUNCH DUTY

- Report for duty at time specified.
- Basic responsibility is to supervise the students to ensure that acceptable standards of student behavior and safety are maintained—strive for room cleanliness.
- Circulate throughout the cafeteria urging students to return all plates and silverware and to clean up all debris. Use a firm, but reasonable, approach. Be careful about confrontations while the student's peers are watching. Don't hesitate to ask regular staff members to assist in troublesome situations.
- The stage area is off limits to students.
- Students are to be kept away from the window wall (west wall).
- Seniors may be excused to eat their lunch in the senior lounge. If there is doubt as to whether the student is a senior or not, check his/her photo I.D.

PHONE EXTENSIONS

Main Office/Principal's Office 2000

Principal's Office 2001

Nurse's Office 2002

Guidance Office 2011

(continued)

(Continued)

Page 6

STUDY HALL

- Report to the assigned responsibility in time to receive students.
- Take attendance of all students required to attend. Keep list of all in attendance or absentees, if known, for regular teacher as part of end-of-day report.
- Excuse only those students who have a bona fide pass from a staff member and only at beginning of the period.
- Expect the students to settle down and get to work. **A QUIET STUDY** is required.
- Serve as a resource person to students—walk around the room assisting where you can.
- Keep all students in the room the entire period.
- Be watchful for students carrying off materials when they leave.

HEALTH PROCEDURES

In addition to the customary referrals to the school nurse for handling minor health problems, your attention is directed to the teacher's desk where a pair of special medical gloves has been provided for the handling of body fluids which may have a negative effect on the personal well-being of you as a substitute and the others in the building.

Basically, when handling bodily fluids such as blood loss, student vomiting, etc., proper caution should be taken with the loss of fluids so that skin contact can be alleviated. After using gloves, place in manila envelope, staple and discard. Wash your hands thoroughly. More thorough instructions on how to handle these emergencies may be obtained through the school nurse during the day.

Page 7

A second set of site-specific information comes from Dr. Virginia Newlin, national board–certified teacher (NBCT) and principal at Rock Hall Middle School in Maryland. The first artifact is a substitute binder that teachers are required to compile for what Dr. Newlin calls "visiting teachers." This binder is even more specific than a generic school handbook because it is teacher-specific and teacher-generated.

SCHOOL ARTIFACT

SUBSTITUTE BINDER

Each teacher will maintain a three-ring substitute binder in the office with up-to-date information.

I. In the office: due by Friday, August 25th.

All items should be put in plastic sheet protectors.

The following sections (use tabs) should be provided:

Section I: Schedules

Complete personal schedule with times and all duties (including locker/hall)

RHMS Master Schedule

Bell Schedule

AM/PM Staff Duties

Section II: Procedures

Complete explanations of all procedures

Handing in homework, taking attendance, bathroom procedures, breakfast & lunch, etc.

Bus groups & bus/dismissal procedures

Section III: Class lists & seating charts

Up-to-date class lists and seating charts for all classes

Be sure to include advisory & A&E groups.

Section IV: Lesson Plans for Day of Absence

This section will be empty until you are out, except for sponge activities. Include the location in your classroom of needed supplies.

Include sponge activities in case your lesson plans do not take the whole period.

Section V: Emergency Procedures

School floor plan with your room, the fire exit, and the teacher's lounge clearly marked

Fire drill & tornado drill procedures

Code red & code green drill procedures

Section VI: Miscellany

The name of a buddy teacher close by

The names of two helpful students in each class

The school map with the fire exit for your classroom & teacher's lounge clearly marked

List of any special directions that involve individual students

Section VI: Emergency Lesson Plans

This must include **unused** lesson plans for each class you teach.

(Include the location in your classroom of needed supplies.)

In this short and to-the-point second artifact from Dr. Newlin, she welcomes the "visiting teachers" and bids them a great day while providing a more general set of schedule guidelines and information above and beyond information in the teacher-assembled binder.

SCHOOL ARTIFACT

Rock Hall Middle School
21203 Sharp Street
P.O. Box 719
Rock Hall, Maryland 21661

GUIDELINES FOR VISITING TEACHERS AT ROCK HALL MIDDLE SCHOOL

Welcome!

1. Arrive at 8:25 AM AT THE LATEST—Students arrive at 8:30, so you might want a little more time than this to get yourself organized.

2. Check in at the office with Mrs. Manley for daily plans. (Plans & materials may also be on the teacher's desk.)

3. Proceed to AM duty area to greet students—Check in with a teacher in a nearby room.

   Bell Schedule

   8:30 AM students arrive

   8:45 Homeroom—take attendance before the 9:00 A.M. bell

   9:00 AM instruction begins

   In order for consistency and continuity of instruction to take place, it is imperative that teacher plans be followed as closely as possible.

4. In general, you should not need to issue students hall passes. However, if you feel it is absolutely necessary, put the student's name, the date, the time, the destination, and your name on the pass. If there are any concerns, please call the principal or the teacher in charge.

5. Students have the opportunity for bathroom breaks during breakfast, lunch, gym, and at-dismissal time.

   Grades 5 & 6 have scheduled breaks mid-morning and afternoon.

   Grades 7 & 8 use restrooms at class changes.

6. Grades 5 & 6 must be escorted to and from specials and lunch.

7. Grades 7 & 8 change classes on their own. However, 7th & 8th grades are walked to the ramp at lunch and picked up after lunch at the cafeteria.

8. Please check the posted fire drill plan for evacuation of the building located next to the classroom door. Be sure to take a class roster with you as you exit the building.

9. Students must be supervised at all times. Do not leave them unattended! If you need to leave the room, send a student to or call the office.

10. Instruction begins promptly and continues to the end of the class. All students must remain seated at all times. Students are dismissed from the classroom at the bell by the teacher.
11. Follow dismissal procedures provided by the teacher.
12. If you need any assistance, please ask the teacher nearest to your room.
13. During the teacher planning time please check with the office to see if your assistance is needed elsewhere in the building.

Have a great day!

Gather Basic Resources and Supplies

The first day of subbing in a school is like any other, whether you are new to subbing or a thirty-year veteran who is returning to sub, and, if you are well prepared, the day will pass very quickly, and you will be on to the next subbing assignment!

Success of the Day Journal

Keep a "Success of the Day" Journal. Buy yourself a blank journal, and then write the date and three successes of each subbing experience. It might be that your class responded favorably to a particular lesson. Your principal may have complimented you on how well your class behaved during a walk-through, or a colleague may have told you how excited your students were after the period ended. Or a parent may have commented on how she wishes you would be her child's teacher next school year. This will become your reflective journal. Initially you should only write down successes. Later, you can add suggestions for improvement as you reflect on your day. You will find that rereading the journal at the end of each week will be written proof to you that you know what you are doing.

Include in your journal space to write down specific room environment ideas, lesson plans, management systems, discipline plans, bulletin boards, and assorted other impressions that you can carry with you to your own teaching position.

Day Planner

Keep a day planner/calendar or electronic organizer. You probably use some sort of calendar, date book, or electronic organizer to keep track of upcoming events in your life. Now you need to think about a planner in which you list subbing assignments and events surrounding them.

Just-in-Case Kit

Keep a personal "just-in-case kit" in your backpack or tote bag with items such as a change of socks or hose, a toothbrush and toothpaste, sewing kit,

Retired Teacher/Substitute Speaks...

Even more important than the lesson plans prepared by the regular teacher is the preparation of myself. This I do by having clothing (layered and comfortable) and all materials laid out at night, arranging for a full night of sleep, eating a sturdy breakfast including protein. On the way out the door, I add a TV dinner to supplement the nuts and fruit that I always keep on hand. I allow extra time for travel. Beginning my day quietly and peacefully helps me to arrive ready and relaxed.

Betty Rosentrater

Band-Aids, aspirin, deodorant, light cologne, spare change, snacks, breath mints, and so on. If there is a chance you may be subbing in a messy subject like art or chemistry or in an early grade, you may want a change of shirt or blouse in case of accidental spills. You may want to keep an extra sweater and an umbrella in your tote along with a few snack bars in case you need lunchtime to regroup for the afternoon. Think of this as your school emergency/substitute teacher survival kit.

Introduction Props

Gather a few props to help introduce yourself to the class. You might include photos of pets or hobbies or a list of favorite books. The items you choose to share will serve as visuals when you introduce yourself. I might use a horseshoe, an egg, and a toy mouse to let young students know that I have horses, chickens, and cats as pets.

Basic Supplies

Gather some materials and supplies for your potential students. You don't want to spend precious time searching for teacher supplies when you arrive in your classroom. The teacher may have locked them up in a closet or you may need to do a major search for them. You can stock up on student supplies at discount or warehouse stores.

- Writing paper
- Scissors
- Stapler and staples
- Construction paper
- Blank overhead transparency and markers
- File folders
- Glue sticks

Retired Teacher/Substitute Speaks...

A bag with extra pen and pencil, a special book to share, backup activities, and a small conversation piece make up my "emergency kit." Being ready avoids the stress and mistakes caused by rushing. Leaving home a few minutes early gives a better chance of finding a good parking place, having time to acclimate to the classroom organization, and getting acquainted with the lesson plans, class rituals, and procedures. Thus fortified I'm ready to greet the students with composure and confidence.

Betty Rosentrater

- Colored pencils, pens, and markers
- Paper clips
- Tape
- Rubber bands
- Art supplies such as watercolor sets
- Certificates of achievement, behavior awards, stickers, coupons, small trinkets for behavior management, "good work" stamps, motivational devices, and so on

Apply It!

Ask at least three veteran substitute teachers how they prepare for their assignments. Every substitute teacher, new and experienced, can always use some fresh ideas. Make a list of relevant, useful, and constructive advice and keep adding to the list as you pick up more tips along the way.

Organize, Organize, Organize

Because you will have limited time to get it together the morning of your assignment, make sure to have all your materials organized at the ready. Identify a place for your subbing materials so you can grab what you need in a flash. You don't want to start the day with a frenzied search for your stuff. Subbing is anxiety producing in itself, so you want to alleviate the need to make it even more so.

The Loose-Leaf Binder

Buy a big loose-leaf binder to organize all your materials. Insert dividers that have pockets for loose materials and tab the dividers with labels such as these:

- School information, including school secretary in charge of calling
- Maps of school sites
- Directions to school sites

- Calendar
- Subbing assignments/log
- Financial records or pay stubs
- Great ideas and terrific bulletin boards (take photos)
- Blank commendations and certificates for students
- Blank summaries/evaluations of the day
- Blank hall or library passes
- Blank seating charts
- Copies of sub instructions from teachers who provide them
- Copies of lesson plans organized by grade or subject from www.lessonplanspage.com
- Copies of substitute teacher tips
- Top-notch lesson plan ideas
- Classroom management ideas if you plan on teaching
- Photos of classroom environments/seating options if you plan on teaching

Prepare Supplemental Materials

As a sub you are expected to follow the teacher's plans to the letter. But having some backup is essential in case lesson plans are too vague, don't last through the day, or are missing altogether. Your supplemental materials box or bag should be stocked with new and different materials that pertain to your subject or subjects and supplements the plans you may or may not find in the classroom. It might include a History Channel video for an American history class, play scripts for an English class, an experiment for a middle school science class, or special arts or crafts projects and one-minute mysteries for elementary students. Chapter 15 talks more about how to plan for the possibility of nonexistent or incomplete plans. You might want to take a peek at that chapter now.

One veteran retired teacher, who is now a two-days-a-week substitute teacher, has a well-stocked and labeled tote bag for every grade level. He just grabs the appropriate bag on his way out the door and if he doesn't need it, fine. But if he finds no plans or inappropriate plans, he is set for the day.

Retired Teacher/Substitute Speaks...

Be prepared with stories to read to class, a simple art project, and a simple writing assignment. I sub only at three grade levels. I have plans for a full day of teaching should I be left on my own.

Anne Sandel

Apply It!

As soon as you know what your assignments may be, begin to stock a "just-in-case" bag. As you add more and more grade levels or subjects you can prepare new bags. In no time you will have a shelf of instant teaching materials to grab on your way out the door.

Extra Teacher's Guide

If you are a one-subject sub, ask for an extra copy of the teacher's edition of the text you will be working with. This is the best way you can adequately prepare your curriculum. Many teacher materials can be complex. So you will need time before the day begins to get the big picture of all you are

Teacher Talks...

I'm currently a fourth-grade teacher in my sixth year with this grade. I have a great pool of substitute teachers who work with me. • Found a new one this year. Actually she found me. Talk about a woman with a plan and a purpose. Ms. R signed up for my classroom online and immediately e-mailed me at my school e-mail to ask if there was anything she could do to prepare for her day with my students. I was impressed. I actually was able to e-mail my sub plans to Ms. R. early and she was able to prepare herself for a successful day. We exchanged a few e-mails and I felt good about leaving my students in her hands. •• Ms. R. has been proactive with staying in touch, and I knew right away she was someone I wanted to prearrange. The first time Ms. R. subbed for me was a success for behavior management. She used the list of students given to her from the office and wrote in pluses and minuses throughout the day, telling the students that was what she was doing. It worked for her! My students responded well overall. •• Ms. R. has communicated with me via e-mail several times. When I was out for 3 days, we were so well established as partners that I hadn't one worry about leaving my students. I knew they were in good hands. Ms. R. came by before I left, borrowed the core literature book so she could read it, and went over plans so we could address questions. Ms. R is flexible, enthusiastic, and energetic and loves kids and teaching. She is a true find and I hope she will be working in our district as a full-time employee by next year! P.S. Ms. R. has maintained a very professional relationship with the teachers she works with. She goes beyond by sending well wishes and happy holidays e-cards and cards. She's doing all the right things! A teacher's dream. :)•

Lori Rozelle

expected to cover that day. Skimming the manual will also give you time to think of additional strategies or activities you can use in your lessons. If you are a long-term substitute teacher, you have the luxury of taking books home to prepare for the days ahead.

This is as far as you can go without knowing exactly what grades or subjects you are subbing in. Think of this chapter as the big picture for any sub. In the next chapter you will begin to think about professional dress and behavior and the attitude you project.

CHAPTER 4

Dressing and Behaving Professionally

Effectiveness Essentials

- Maintain a positive and confident frame of mind.

- Dress professionally.

- Make your first impression a lasting one.

- Project a confident, business-as-usual attitude.

- Be engaged with students at all times.

Prior to your first assignment, consider your inner and outer wardrobe. How will you present yourself to the students? How will you appear to *them*? Will you project confidence and competence? Will you dress like someone who means business? A subbing assignment requires that you be engaged at all times with instruction, oversight, and assistance. This is not your time for catching up on your own work.

Dress Professionally

Don't

Do

Professional dress will help with classroom discipline. When you dress casually, the students perceive you as being casual and may not take you as seriously as they should. Model the dress of the principal or administrators to be on the safe side. You need not run out to a color consultant or buy a dress-for-success manual. A few low-cost upgrades to your wardrobe will give you confidence. Try for the "business casual" look.

Even if "all the other teachers are wearing them," save your sweats and shorts for the gym and your flip-flops and backless shoes for the weekend. Think about how midriff-baring tops and very short skirts will play in your classroom, especially when you lean over. Although jeans are worn at some schools, your students will be wearing them, and you want to distinguish yourself from them. Students will make judgments about you as soon as they enter the room, and you can gain an advantage in the respect department by dressing as if you deserve it. Dressing professionally is essential for all teachers, but since some students may view you as a "babysitter," the clothes you wear should convey the impression that you mean business and that work will go on as usual.

MYTH BUSTER!

Students Like a Teacher (or Substitute) Who Is With It and Relates to Them as a Peer

I remember the principal of the school where I did my practice teaching 30 years ago reminding me that the students have friends; they do not need me to be their friend—they need me to be their teacher. That means compassion, wisdom, and experience on my part, but I do not need to be their buddy.

Beth Ann Willstrop
Grades 9–12
English and reading

Plan what you will wear on subbing days to look your professional best. You will feel more confident, and those you encounter will make judgments about your professionalism based solely on your looks, rightly or wrongly, since they have no other data. Consider what message you want to send to others and let that be a guiding principle of how you dress.

Balance professional dress with comfort. While some veteran subs suggest a dressy dress or suit and tie on subbing day, most stress comfort. You will have to take into consideration climate, school norms, and grade level as well as your own personal taste. Sitting on the floor or handling paints and paste may dictate more casual clothing or, better yet, a smock that suits you. Think about your poor feet, too! Wear comfortable shoes!

It's okay to be a little playful. Wearing subject-related clothing shows you have a sense of playfulness while being professional. This might be a tie with global themes or a dress with a book pattern. Science subs might wear a lab coat. You can accessorize with scarves or pins to advertise your subject areas. One elementary sub is known around the school for her "cool" socks that coordinate with her outfits. Another sub has a sweater for major holidays. But in high school, especially, don't overdo the playfulness lest you be considered weird or "dorky."

MYTH BUSTER!

How a Substitute Teacher Dresses Is Not Important

The kids notice everything about you. My high school students commented on every aspect of my clothes, nails, shoes, hair. All teachers are idols until they prove themselves otherwise. Don't try to look like your students. It rings false for them. They don't want another peer because they are struggling with peer relationships as it is and you can be the bellwether of fine fashion for them. Keep the sweats in your gym bag. Dress comfortably but do dress up. I always feel better about myself when I look my best.

Dottie Bailey
Speech therapist/teacher

Project Confidence in Your Introduction

You can no doubt remember your first public speaking experience. It might have been the first time you made a speech, stood up to read a poem, stood before your class to read a passage, or participated in a play or debate. You probably felt as if you would freeze up or wanted to run off to hide. The reality is that you are well prepared to address your first class as a substitute teacher. Your students will likely not remember what you said first, but because it is of primary concern to new substitute teachers, here are some common introductions:

The Welcomers attempt to make the student feel right at home and set a positive tone at the outset.

"Good morning. Your teacher, _____, will not be here today and I am your substitute teacher, _____. I'm here to save the day for learning."

"I am your substitute teacher and we are going to have a great day together."

"I am Mr._____, your chemistry sub, and we will be following your teacher's plan this period."

The Managers put classroom management, rules, and discipline right out there and convey the expectation that the class will be well organized and well behaved.

"The line is very straight, and I appreciate how quietly everyone entered the room."

"I am your substitute teacher, _____, and I know you will make your teacher proud."

Other unique first words offered by substitute teachers include, "I'm happy and excited to be your substitute teacher today. My own children go to this school and I am very familiar with the routine."

"I may look familiar to some of you. I retired last year but came back to this school because I missed teaching so much."

Secondary students may not remember what you said first, but they will be evaluating you on the "cool" and professional scales. Younger students may express their concerns differently, but all students will be more concerned with the issues that directly affect them than with your first words. They will want to know if you will follow the teacher's plan, whether you know the classroom rules and plan to enforce them, and whether they will still have homework. Deep inside, however, students of any age are curious about your personal life, and you should share something with them.

It is most appropriate to be called by your last name preceded by Mr., Mrs., or Ms. These are customary titles and they convey professional respect. Many middle and high school teachers call on their students using these titles and the students' last names to convey mutual respect. In all cases, write your name on the chalkboard, pronounce it with the students, and have them repeat it. During attendance in elementary school, ask students to respond to your salutation, "Good morning, Juan" with "Good morning, Mr. _____." In many middle and high schools, attendance is taken by a student teaching assistant (T.A.) who uses the class list on a computer spreadsheet to identify absentees. He or she knows who is absent and this obviates the need to call the roll. However, use the seating chart to establish contact at the outset.

A little disclosure goes a long way. Tell your students something about your personal life and professional background. You can tell the students about your family, pets, hobbies, why you are a substitute teacher, and, if you know, why the teacher is not in school this day and when he or she will return.

Apply It!

Make up these envelopes in advance and hand them out to your students to convey how you will operate. Convey your goals for the day to your students with a survival sack or small manila envelope that contains items such as these and has the icon of a lifesaver buoy to remind them that you are here to save the day for learning. You can collect them at the end of the period or day and reuse them.

Object	Meaning
Rubber band	Be flexible in adapting to the sub.
Paper clip	Stay connected in your teacher's absence.
Eraser	Everyone makes mistakes.
Sticky note	We will stick to your teacher's plans today.
Lifesaver candy	Substitutes save the day for learning.
Piece of string	Remember to make your teacher proud.

You will have to contain any apprehension you are feeling lest it be communicated to the students. Many of them will be flummoxed by their regular teacher's absence, and you are the one who has to comfort and reassure them that work will go on as usual. You can best do this by taking a deep breath, standing up tall, and conveying to them that you are experienced, well prepared, and confident that the day will go smoothly. You may have to do your best acting job, but never let them know how nervous you may really feel.

Behaving Professionally

Your time in the classroom should be focused entirely on the students. You are there to continue the instructional program in the teacher's absence, and you are being paid to make sure that the day is spent on learning.

> ## Principal's Perspective...
>
> *Always be courteous and respectful, but firm. DO NOT try to be a friend!*
>
> *Never leave the students unattended. If you need help, use the classroom call button or send a trustworthy student to the office.*
>
> *Never talk outside of school about what you learned/saw/heard in school. What you learn about students is confidential and anyway, you wouldn't want some stranger talking about your child. If you have a specific concern, discuss it with the guidance counselor and/or principal.*
>
> *Follow the instructions left by the teacher as carefully as possible. Nothing annoys a teacher more than to find a substitute has not covered the material as instructed and, as a result, he or she has to make up lost instructional time.*
>
> *Dr. Virginia Newlin, NBCT*
> *Principal, Rock Hill Middle School*

Behaving Professionally with Self-Starters

I have been in many well-run classes in middle and high school where the students know exactly what to do in their teacher's absence. They get right down to assignments and the sub has "very little" instructional input. In fact, I have been in classes where the students are so well trained that, with no sub present, the students would get to work. They are graded by their regular teacher and get points for completing assignments, so they do not tend to goof off.

However, when you find yourself in such a situation, you are not off the hook. There is never a reason to use your cell phone for personal calls, to read the newspaper, to knit, to use the computers for non-school-related purposes, to drink coffee, to eat snacks, and so on. If the students are self-starters, walk around and look for students who seem off-task or distracted or need help.

Behaving Professionally in General

In most situations, you will not have time to engage in noninstructional activities such as the ones described above. You will be moving all around the room, instructing, helping, overseeing, and so forth. In elementary classrooms you will find yourself in constant motion, and this will be true in secondary classrooms as well when the plans call for you to either provide input or keep things moving along and under control. If you have some down time, it is still unprofessional to engage in your own personal chores or diversions.

Teacher Talks…

Do not say anything negative about the way the classroom is organized or procedures that are in place, and so on. That will undermine the "regular" teacher when she or he returns and it will not "win friends." You want to be called back to that school and you'll eventually come face to face with the "regular" teacher. Just remember, whatever you say in the classroom doesn't stay in the classroom . . . it's not Las Vegas.

J. P. Stein
Educational coach

Make sure that you are businesslike at all times and do not engage in physical responses that may be interpreted as inappropriate. Some students will misconstrue the hand on a shoulder or any other touching, so it is best to avoid even the appearance of impropriety.

Act like the professional you are and never convey a chumminess with the students. They want someone who is a teacher, not a friend. Although I know a sub who lets the students call her "grandma," in lieu of her last name, this is highly unusual and results from her working in only a few schools where she is well known and once taught.

You can convey your role as a substitute teacher by your dress, demeanor, behavior, and words. The clothing and words you choose often determine how much respect and status your students accord you. Facial piercings and tattoos may be acceptable in some circles but remove piercings and cover tattoos during the work week.

Avoid It!

Never make fun of or demean any of the students to other teachers, the administrator, or your friends. Maintain confidentiality at all times. The woman standing next to you at the supermarket may be the mother of the student you are describing to your friend. Even if you have a funny anecdote that is basically harmless, avoid talking about the students you encounter.

Now that you are dressed and well-prepared professionally, it's time to learn the basic principles of subbing. Read on.

CHAPTER 5

Ten Basic Principles for a Successful Subbing Experience

Effectiveness Essentials

- Preparation and motivation will make your day go smoothly.

- Maintain the teacher's routines, procedures, and discipline policy.

- Flexibility, professionalism, and self-confidence are key.

- Promote a successful and positive experience for the students.

Guiding Principle	Message Sent to Students
1. Be overprepared.	The sub has it all together.
2. Motivate.	The day will be fun as well as productive.
3. Maintain routines.	The sub knows our routines.
4. Maintain rules.	Today is not party time.
5. Be flexible.	The sub reassures us.
6. Be confident.	We can't put anything over on this sub.
7. Adopt a professional demeanor.	The sub is not trying too hard to be liked.
8. Be aware and alert.	The sub can spot trouble.
9. Acknowledge students.	The sub enjoys his or her job.
10. Be clear and review.	The sub makes things easy to understand.

Ten basic principles can guide you to a successful subbing experience. Incorporating and following these principles will give you a sense of control over your first day of subbing and beyond. Each principle conveys an important message to students that will help set the tone for the day or for your long-term subbing experience.

Be Overprepared

Arrive very early. As soon as you know your assigned school and grade level, head out the door. You will feel more confident if you can spend time before class checking out the room and feeling comfortable in it. Make sure your name is on the board along with the daily schedule or the schedule for the period. The one certainty for the first day is that you will forget to do something! Writing the outline of activities or schedule on the board will serve as a cueing device for you and a reminder to your students that you are well organized and have given a great deal of thought to this day. After consulting the plans, have all your instructional materials at the ready.

> *Message Sent to Students:* This substitute teacher has put effort into this day or period and really is businesslike. She knows what she is about and has thought this through. This substitute teacher doesn't "wing it." So I better not fool around.

Motivate

When students realize that their teacher is absent, they may think that the sub is just there to fill time. You want to dispel that notion very quickly. Prepare a simple activity to let them know that this day might even be fun!

One activity that requires no work or advance preparation beyond knowing the grade level is a "Magic" box guessing game. The box will contain something related to the schoolwork. You can pick up any object around the room and put it in your "Magic" box. The students have to guess what you have hidden following these simple rules:

1. Ask only questions that I can answer with yes or no.
2. Listen and do not repeat questions already asked.
3. Everyone gets a turn.
4. If you think you know, do not call out but write it on a sticky note.
5. Reveal the object when everyone has had a chance.

> ***Message Sent to Students:*** This class will be exciting. The substitute teacher has made an effort to convey that he will do the utmost to keep things moving along so we won't be bored.

Apply It!

In all grades, including high school, let the students know that you have something in your Supplement Materials Bag or Tote that you think they will enjoy when all the work is finished. What will yours be?

Maintain Routines/Schedules

You may have to establish your own routines if the teacher has not provided detailed information regarding lining up, procedures for collecting papers, bathroom procedures, and so on. You will need to read Chapters 9 and 10 carefully, both of which discuss possible routines at length. You have to be prepared for "Mr._____doesn't do it that way" with the response, "Yes, I know, but we are trying this new way that always works just as well." Routines are the tools for saving time and ensuring smooth functioning, structure, and security.

> ***Message Sent to Students:*** This sub is organized and knows how we do things in this class. The sub may even have a more organized approach than our teacher.

Teacher Talks...

The role of the sub is to keep the class on track/on the same schedule as if the teacher was there. One has to be adaptable and willing to work with children to be a sub. Thick skin is a must. Be ready for "Mr. Peterson doesn't do that."

Michael Peterson
First grade

Maintain Classroom Rules

No matter what grade level or subject matter you sub in, you will need to reinforce the classroom rules or, in the absence of any on the board or poster around the room, make up your own. You will have an opportunity to learn about rule making in Chapter 11. Choose a few key rules and stick to them. They should convey a positive discipline system based on mutual respect, responsibility, and dignity. Don't let infractions slide! Thirty pairs of eyes (or more!) will be watching!

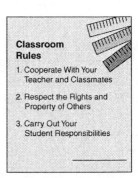

Classroom Rules

1. Cooperate With Your Teacher and Classmates
2. Respect the Rights and Property of Others
3. Carry Out Your Student Responsibilities

> *Message Sent to Students:* I will be safe and I will be responsible for my actions. This is not party time, and the sub is not a pushover.

stop.

Be Flexible

Recognize that students will be apprehensive about having a sub and about your expectations for them. They may be concerned about their teacher's absence and whether this is a long-term situation or just a day. You need to provide the structure and reassurance that will allay their fears. Recognize that they may show their discomfort and anxiety by acting out. The way to counter this is by showing them that you know what you are doing and that the day will be a fun and productive one.

> *Message Sent to Students:* No need to worry. The sub knows her way around the school and the classroom.

Be Confident

If you have ever been in an unfamiliar situation, you know how important it is to assess the situation quickly by looking around the environment and making some key observations about what is going on. That is exactly what you need to do when you first enter the classroom. Check out the room, including any posted rules, the seating arrangement, the posters around the room, the bulletin boards, the shelves and books they hold. "What goes on here normally?" is the question you should first ask yourself. Then look for the instructions, if any, the teacher has left you to confirm your impressions. Finally, look over the plans that will help you figure out what should happen during the day or period. Once you make your on-the-spot assessment, adopt an attitude of, "This is a snap." The students will sense your confident attitude and will be less likely to take advantage of you.

> ***Message Sent to Students:*** We can't put anything over on this sub. He seems to know what he is doing.

Adopt a Professional Demeanor

No matter what your age and experience in teaching, you need to adopt a businesslike demeanor when you enter the classroom. That means being

Teacher Talks...

Don't come into a classroom that you are unfamiliar with being too hard or strict. Kids don't like change so you need to feel out how the class is normally run and then figure out what works best for you. Don't be too easy either or they will walk all over you. Try to become a regular sub for teachers that you like or a regular at a specific school.

Barbara Arient
High school special educator

Student Says...

When we have an inexperienced substitute teacher, the class goes nuts. The students know they can get away with it because the subs act like big kids. When we have a sub who knows the ropes, students try to get away with it but they don't succeed. The students can tell who is strict and who isn't in five minutes. Experienced subs act like professionals.

Natalie, age 18
High school senior

firm, yet friendly, but not too chummy. You need to strike a balance between being firm, yet fair.

Message Sent to Students: This sub is not trying too hard to be liked.

Be Aware and Alert

If you learn one skill prior to subbing, it should be how to have eyes in the back of your head and how to be consistent in enforcing rules and procedures. Your students will be waiting for you to make a mistake, any mistake, and to pull the wool over your eyes. You need to show at the outset that you can anticipate trouble. You will want to use the techniques suggested in Chapter 12, especially the nonverbal techniques of proximity control, to make sure that you nip any misbehaviors in the bud.

Message Sent to Students: This sub can spot trouble.

Acknowledge Students

Let each student know with a verbal or nonverbal response from you that she or he is valued and special. It can start with individual greetings to students on their way into the room. A greeting in the primary language of second-language learners will make them feel welcome. Ask students to make nameplates out of folded index cards that you provide or use the seating chart to call on students by name. Use the blank commendations to give out throughout the day. They can lead to a trip to the trinket box or just serve as positive reinforcers. As you walk around the room, liberally compliment the students on their efforts.

Message Sent to Students: This sub likes her job and has respect for students.

Student Says...

What should a sub know about kids? That they are nice kids. She or he should know our names.

Drew, age 8
Third grade

Be Clear and Review

Students should go home after having you as a sub feeling that they have accomplished something. Step in when you see that a given task is too difficult or frustrating. Although you have lesson plans to follow, make sure

Student Says...

When my normal teacher is teaching math she doesn't use the problems out of the book, she gives us easier problems so we learn better. She explains the problems so we learn to do them faster and easier. The substitute teacher just makes us copy and do the work out of the book. It's harder, it can be frustrating, and sometimes we don't get it.

Walker, age 11
Sixth grade

Retired Teacher/Substitute's Additional Four Principles

1. Humor
Go into the classroom assuming you will have a good time. Kids can spot someone who genuinely wants to be there and someone who is just in it for the money. A sense of humor always helped me during the bad times of teaching and it has served me well in substituting. Kids of all ages love a teacher who is comfortable with them and sees humor even during the bad times.

2. Patience
Maintain a patient attitude, especially with younger ones and those who are "behaviorally challenged." Don't lose your cool. Be in control.

3. Be Prepared
Even though there are lesson plans, they don't always work out. You may have time on your hands. Be prepared to fill in those "holes" with some educational/fun games you can play with them, either orally or on the whiteboard. I have a few that I have accumulated that work with different grade levels and don't require any materials. For upper-grade classes, for example, I like to play a digit-place game on the whiteboard. For lower-grade classes, I like to play simple games such as "I Spy."

4. Motivate Them
Have a "carrot" you can dangle that they can look forward to—if they behave. I like to play Bingo with them at the end of the day with simple prizes for winners. Even promising to read a favorite book at the end of the day can be motivation for younger children. Older kids always want P.E. so you can promise to extend P.E. time.

Sally Steinbrunn

that you adapt the work when you sense that it is too hard for the students. You can even ask them to turn to the last chapter in their text and play some sort of review game with them. See Chapter 13 for some easy-to-use strategies to review work.

Message Sent to Students: This sub makes the work easy to understand.

When you keep all these principles in mind, they will serve as a framework for the material that follows in this book. They provide a big picture of your role as a substitute teacher, and you can review them again and again before any new assignment.

CHAPTER 6

How Teachers Prepare for Subs

Effectiveness Essentials

- The substitute folder provides a wealth of important information.

- Teachers should emphasize respect for substitute teachers.

- There are simple remedies if the sub folder is incomplete.

Teachers who want to return to a class that has spent productive time in their absence make every effort to prepare informative materials as well as complete and detailed plans for the substitute. Conscientious teachers also prepare their students for substitute teachers so that subs are accorded the same respect as the teachers they pinch-hit for.

Teachers want to ensure that learning takes place in their absence. They don't want to have to pick up the pieces when they return to school, nor do they want to stay at home with the flu feeling guilty about what might be going on in their absence. Conscientious teachers make key preparations to prepare for your substituting experience. Here are some common documents and items you can expect to find in a prominent place in the classroom.

The Substitute Folder

Teachers know that the more information the substitute teacher has about the class, the procedures, and the schedule, the better the sub will handle the other ambiguities. This information is usually in concise form because the teachers know that substitutes may arrive five minutes before class and will not have much time to prepare. Meticulous teachers provide a

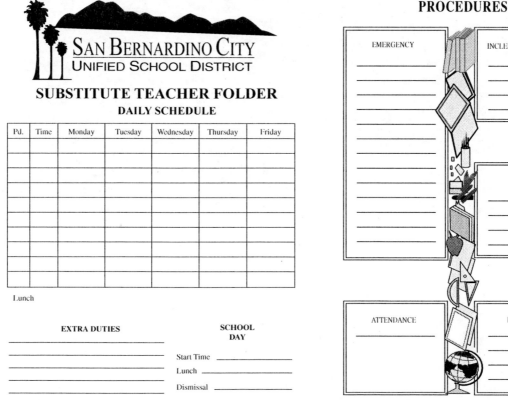

Figure 6.1   Substitute Folder

Figure 6.2   School Procedures

Used with permission of the San Bernardino City Unified School District, Superintendent Dr. Arturo Delgado, and Principal Kenneth Martinez.

Names	Period _____	Attendance

Figure 6.3 Class Roster

bright-colored folder clearly marked for you so you can find it without calling out the bloodhounds. In Chapter 3, there is a complete substitute folder that the principal, Dr. Newlin, requires every teacher to prepare using the same format. If there is no schoolwide template, look for a substitute folder in the classroom. The folder should be clearly marked.

The folder often contains the following data.

- *Multiple Copies of the Class List.*   This is an easy way for the substitute to make notations of all sorts and check off the homework.
- *Seating Chart.*   A seating chart will help you learn the names or at least call on the students with ease. The seating chart will also help you to quickly catch those who decide to pull a switcheroo and sit with a friend for the day. If your teacher really wants to ensure no one changes places, he or she can insert small digital photos of the students along with the names on the seating chart.
- *School Map.*   You can obtain a map of the school site from the office, but teachers often leave one in the substitute folder so you can easily find key school locations.
- *Class Schedule and Comings and Goings.*   Teachers often provide a general class schedule and schedule of out-of-room activities. This schedule includes days and times. There is often much confusion about comings and goings, and 35 voices expressing conflicting accounts of when they have library can be most distressing to the already harried substitute.
- *Bell Schedule/Lunch/Recess/Dismissal.*

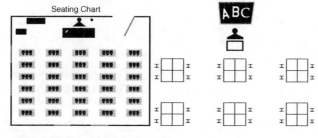

Figure 6.4 Seating Charts

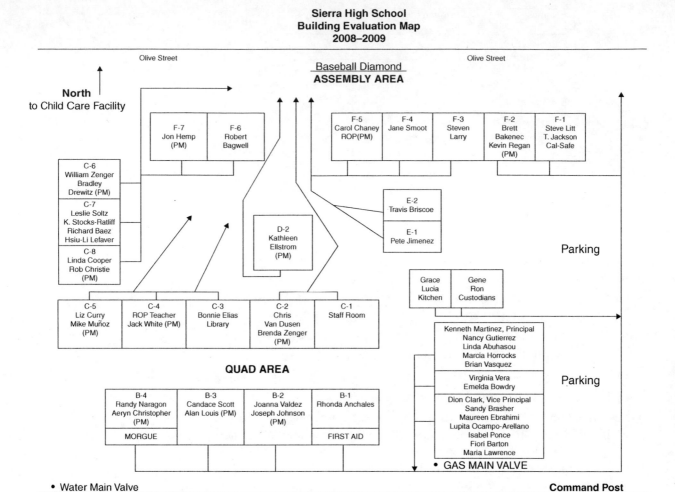

Figure 6.5   School Map

Used with permission of the San Bernardino City Unified School District, Superintendent Dr. Arturo Delgado, and Principal Kenneth Martinez.

- *Emergency Procedures.*
- *Summary of Administrative Duties by Day.*   Substitutes are expected to follow the teacher's schedule exactly, and they need to know what extra school duties need coverage. The teacher(s) you sub for should change this schedule monthly, since teacher duties change from month to month.
- *Discipline and Organization.*   Teachers should provide information about their discipline plan. The most well-organized teachers include the letter regarding discipline that has been sent home to parents or was included in the course syllabus. You can ascertain the rules from this letter, and the same rules are usually posted prominently in the room.
- *Welcome Letter.*   Very often the principal includes a letter to subs welcoming them, thanking them, and articulating specific schoolwide procedures.

Sierra High School
2008–09

Regular Day Schedule

Morning Session

Period	Time (am)
1	7:55–9:25
Break/Passing	
2	9:38–11:05
Break/Passing	
3	11:18–12:45
Dismissal	12:45
Lunch	12:45–1:20

Regular Day Schedule

2nd Session

Period	Time (pm)
Lunch	12:55–1:30
4	1:30–3:00
Break/Passing	
5	3:13–4:40
Break/Passing	
6	4:53–6:20
Dismissal	6:20

I hereby certify that the above information is true and correct.

_____   _____
Principal's Signature   Date

Figure 6.6   Regular Day Schedule

Used with permission of the San Bernardino City Unified School District, Superintendent Dr. Arturo Delgado, and Principal Kenneth Martinez.

- *Bus Information in Concise Form.*   As a sub you want to make sure that everyone gets on the right bus at the right time.
- *Buddy Teachers, Aides, and Volunteer Schedules.*   Thorough teachers often provide substitutes with the name and room number of a buddy teacher, the name of the aide and the aide's hours, the schedule of any expected volunteers for the day, and the names of three students who can be counted on to give accurate and up-to-the-minute information about classroom life in general. This last bit of information is very important, especially if the aforementioned documents and forms are missing from the sub folder.

Dear Substitute:

Welcome and thank you for spending the day with us at Sierra High School.

In order to help you follow our procedures and not be led astray by some of our more creative students, please be aware of the following:

1. Students must be in the classroom at 7:55 am when the bell rings. If they are not, please send them to the office for a tardy pass.

2. **NO** passes are given the 1st or last 15 minutes of a period.

3. No more than one (1) student leaves the room on a pass at a time.

4. Be certain passes have the complete student name, your name, and the time the student left the room. No passes are given to use the phone.

5. Absolutely **No** videos are to be shown. Please notify the principal immediately if the teacher has left instructions to show a video.

6. Substitute teachers are expected to follow the instructions left by the regular teacher. Please do not substitute your own lesson.

7. If at any time you have a question or concern, please call the office (Dial 226). We will assist you promptly. While students may think they know, please check with the office.

8. If you have an emergency and need to leave the room yourself, call the office. We will have someone cover your class. DO NOT leave students in a classroom unattended!

9. Please follow the bell schedule and wait to dismiss the class when the passing bell rings. DO NOT let students tell you it's time to go.

10. DO NOT leave the classroom unlocked during breaks unless you are remaining in the room. The custodian, security, principal, or vice principal will open the door for you again.

We hope you have a great day here at Sierra HS.

Sincerely,

Kenneth Martinez, Principal

Figure 6.7   Letter from the Principal

Used with permission of the San Bernardino City Unified School District, Superintendent Dr. Arturo Delgado, and Principal Kenneth Martinez.

- *Notations about Students with Special Needs.*   Teachers should be sharing information about students with special needs. Some students may need to see the nurse for medication or diabetic testing. Others may have adaptive P.E. Still others may have modified work programs and different behavior standards.

Some teachers will communicate all this information to subs in a concise fashion, covering the same important information and giving it a name like "Substitute Data Bank."

Substitute Data Bank

Here's what you'll need:	Where you can find it:
Lesson plans	Lesson plan book on teacher's desk
Daily schedule	Lesson plan book on teacher's desk
Additional duties	In notes section of lesson plan book
Grade book	Top drawer of teacher's desk
Attendance	Kept in grade book or on the computer; ask the student T.A. (teaching assistant) or any reliable student
Seating chart	Front of lesson plan book
School map	Office
Emergency procedures	Bulletin board beside teacher's desk
Bus lists	Bulletin board beside teacher's desk
Bell schedule	Bulletin board beside teacher's desk
Emergency information cards	Office

Materials and supplies:	Teacher's desk and storage cabinets
Paper	_____
Pencils	_____
Glue	_____
Tape	_____
Stapler	_____

Procedures

Raising hands	_____
Restroom	_____
Recess	_____
Entrances and exits	_____
Lunch	_____

Students with Special Needs

Names _____ Accommodation _____

Students who get meds from nurse _____ Time _____

Students with allergies _____ Allergy _____

Discipline Policy

A letter outlining the policy is posted inside each student's notebook, signed by the parent. The rules and consequences are written on a poster at the front of the room.

(*continued*)

Key People

Reliable students _____
Buddy teachers _____
Principal _____
Secretary _____
School nurse _____
Resource teachers _____
School counselor _____

Technology

Computers in classroom
and policy for use _____
Other media and equipment _____
Tech-savvy student(s) _____

Weekly Schedule

Teacher Talks...

It will increase your respect (and thereby your return requests and income) if you get to know the classroom you will be working with. Arrive at least 10–15 minutes before the stated time so that you have the opportunity to read the teacher's sub plans thoroughly and allow student leaders to guide you. It will make your day go better.

I leave great substitute teacher plans and I never labor over them for hours the night before. During the third or fourth week of school, after I have figured out the kids and we have established our procedures, I write my sub plans. They are in generic format that I will use for 90% of the days that I am absent. All of the routines and procedures are explicitly typed out. I include every detail of what we are accustomed to (especially with younger classes), things that only the students and I know out of habit because we are there. I leave space to highlight the particulars that change from day to day, like the title of the read-aloud book, the math work that we are on, or special events.

The night before you come to sub, I write in the order of the schedule and highlight the priorities. It leaves me confident that you know exactly what to expect, and yet I have spent the same amount of time planning that I normally do. The final special feature: I ask you to remember that they are children and want to have fun, but also to be very strict so that I get a warm welcome when I return. By getting a feel for the class beforehand that should be an easy task.

Sarah Barten
Kindergarten

Lesson Plans and Supplemental Materials

When teachers know in advance that they will need your services, they leave up-to-the-minute lesson plans and review work for the class. They write plans with the substitute in mind and have all the materials at hand and ready to go. Some teachers, even in an emergency, will quickly write up-to-the-minute plans and send them to school with a friend or spouse that morning.

Lesson plans for subs should be written in a form that would enable any reasonable person to decipher and then teach from them. In addition, teachers who plan ahead for their absence from school include in the substitute folder many review sheets and activities for any possible emergency, and they update the material every two weeks or so just in case.

Teachers often leave the substitute a box or bag of motivating, supplemental activities that they know their students enjoy. With more experience, substitutes will learn to bring their own supplemental materials (Chapter 15). But when classroom teachers provide you with specialized ideas, puzzles, videos, read-aloud books, and activities tailor-made for their class, you can have a much more relaxed experience.

Teacher Talks...

I substituted way back, 20 years ago, when I first got my teaching credential. I was young, smart, and had worked in industry before going into teaching, so I could take on the world. Also, I think kids were a lot easier 20 years ago. Maybe not. Fast forward to 2009: I look for good substitutes for my department (and my own classes), and I usually look for young, high-energy, smart people who can take on the world. I like to get a sub who will keep coming back to our department because we are certainly a different species in that we have computer labs that must be maintained. I prepare my students for a sub. I am very stern about how they are to treat the sub and how they are to do their assigned work or there will be hell to pay when I return. If the sub leaves a student's name, I immediately call the parent, and if the violation was bad enough, I write a conduct referral. In 19 years of teaching I have had to do this 3 times and I remember each time very well. My students know to behave, both with me and with subs. Because of that preparation and the lesson plans I leave, I have subs wanting to come back to my classes; some will only sub for me and my department as we are all pretty much on the same page. On the other hand, because I teach in a very difficult inner city high school, I have heard of subs who have said they will not return or they would never come in the first place. The school has a very bad reputation among subs because of teachers who have not prepared their classes and probably don't have very good classroom management to begin with.

Delaine Zody

Apply It!

What other information would you like to see included in a substitute teacher folder?

Respect for Substitutes

To make substituting easier, many teachers talk to their classes about the role of the substitute teacher and how that person is really an emergency teacher who saves the day for learning. A classroom discipline policy based on a premise of self-responsibility makes it more likely that the students will not take too much advantage of the situation.

It is very important at the secondary level to instill respect for substitute teachers. These students are quite aware that the sub is vulnerable to their monkey business. Teachers should discuss in a meeting with students why they will be absent (if they know ahead of time), rules of behavior, and positive and negative consequences depending on the report they receive from the substitute.

Apply It!

Before you read on, what are some possible solutions if you find no substitute folder and have to start from scratch?

None of the Above

If you enter the room, look hard and long in every nook and cranny, and still find no substitute folder or binder, here are some possible remedies.

No class list	Have the students sign in or look in the class computer. Send a student to the office for a class list. Call the office and have them deliver one.
No seating chart	Start making one. Using a blank seating chart will make the task easier. Have the students fill in their names on the chart. Make sure to keep them busy with a beginning activity while you do this. If you prepare a variety of blank seating chart forms for tables, rows, and round tables, you can easily have them fill in their names or call roll and fill in the names yourself.
No school map	You can often download this from the school Web site, but the office will have copies of the school map for you.

No schedule or agenda	Check the chalkboard or whiteboard first. Teachers often leave this in place from day to day and make small changes. Some teachers post the schedule on a bulletin board.
No bell schedule	Look for bell schedules and lunch and recess break schedules on the bulletin board near the teacher's desk.
No emergency procedure	You should find the emergency procedure in a prominent place on the bulletin board near the teacher's desk.
No administrative duties	Ask during your first break what other duties you are expected to perform in place of the teacher.
No bus schedule	Pass out a paper with columns for walk, bus, stay for after-school activities, and car. Have the students write their names in the proper column.
No discipline policy	Look around the room first. Is there a list of groups and points? Is there a pocket chart with color-coded cards? Is there a set of rules? Is there a warning system of checks with ever-increasing penalties? These are all clues as to the discipline policy in place. If you have no clue, tell the class that their teacher told you the rules and the consequences of breaking them, but you're asking them because you just want to make sure they remember the rules. If you prefer, get the information from a buddy teacher or the teacher next door.
No buddy teacher	Get yourself adopted by a same-grade teacher in close proximity and ask any questions you have.
Students with special needs	It would be very surprising, but not unheard of, if there are no notations regarding individualized education plans (IEPs)—for example, which students go to resource rooms, which ones require that the nurse dispense their medication, which ones are part of inclusion or mainstreaming arrangements, which ones have adaptive P.E., and, in general, which students have modifications of any sort, either physical, behavioral, or instructional. You will need this information from some source and the best one is the resource teacher or the special education coordinator.
No plans	Ask the students what they were studying yesterday and have them turn to those chapters. Quickly get yourself together and ask the "reliable" students to summarize the content and assignments from the day before. This is perhaps the time to take out your supplemental materials.

Retired Teacher Talks...

Now if no plans are available:

1. Each teacher is required to have prepared a week of emergency plans that are usually housed in the office. The school secretary should be able to obtain these for you.
2. Ask the class to choose a leader boy and a leader girl who can tell you the routine and what they are studying. The students will have some comments and teasing, but generally they will pick out the leaders for you. Have these two leaders discuss the past lessons with you publicly and some good ideas will emerge.
3. This is definitely time for your creative genius. Use the class environment and books in the kids' desks to spur you on to a writing activity, even if it's a journal entry with a picture.

Shirley Clark

Teachers who contributed to this chapter are ones who overload the substitute teacher with information. They update the information as things change. It is only in the most severe emergencies that you may find yourself left in the lurch. Teachers are required to leave materials and instructions for substitute teachers, and you can relax and be sure that you will find what you need. If necessary, seek what you need from a colleague, buddy teacher, department chair, resource teacher, or vice principal.

CHAPTER 7

Beginning the Day

Effectiveness Essentials

- Arrive very early and stop in the school office.

- Scope out what the teacher has left for you, including the lesson plans.

- Make some assumptions from the classroom environment.

- Project confidence to your students and keep them busy.

Finally, it's your first day of subbing. You will be ready to go when the phone call comes, whether from the automated system, the sub desk at the district office, or the school secretary. Dress professionally, pack a lunch, and pick up your materials, including your sub binder, your personal emergency kit, your "just-in-case-there-are-no-plans" tote bag, and the supplies you anticipate needing. Then it's out the door with "your right foot forward," as my mother used to say.

Principals' Perspectives...

Plan to arrive half an hour before the students. This time will be invaluable in allowing you to prepare yourself for the day. You will be able to find your way around the school (ask for a quick tour), check out the plans that have been left, check fire drill (or other drill) arrangements, make any necessary copies, and so forth.

Dr. Virginia Newlin
Principal and National Board Certified Teacher

The principal should introduce him- or herself to every substitute in the building every day. I let students know that my expectations are even greater when we have a guest (substitute) in the building. I make sure they know how to call the office and request the assistance of the principal. Students know that if I return, I won't be leaving alone. Substitutes want to be at Pine Grove Elementary School. Substitutes need to know that they have support from the administration, as well as other teachers. As I am in and out of classrooms at least twice a day (AM and PM), my teachers and my substitutes know that I am always a phone call away. One student being sent to the office typically eliminates students trying to put one over on a substitute teacher. I meant by "not leaving alone" that someone will probably be suspended for disrespecting an adult. I tell kids that I only have three expectations for them:

1. Respect yourself and do your best.
2. Respect each other—no bullying, name calling, and so on.
3. Respect all of my staff and adults in this building, not just your teacher.

It's simple and with consistency works at any level.

Richard Weber
Principal, Pine Grove Elementary School

SUBSTITUTE TEACHER TIME CARD

SOC. SEC. NO. _____									

NAME _____   PHONE NO. _____

ADDRESS _____

_____

MONTH _____ 20 _____

DATE	DAYS	PDS	TEACHER SUBSTITUTING FOR	PRIN APPR	ACCOUNT CODE	DAYS	X	RATE	AMOUNT

Figure 7.1   Substitute Teacher Time Card

Arriving at the School

Arrive at the school office on time or, better yet, as early as the school opens. Your first stop should be the school office where you can introduce yourself. Subs will often find their substitute folder in the office. The folder includes documents discussed in previous chapters, including the bell schedule, school map, lunch schedule, emergency procedures, special events, class lists, and so on. Pick up your key to the classroom and head straight there.

In addition to the materials previously described, you may be given detailed instructions for emergencies and policies for fire drills, earthquakes, tornadoes, lockdown, attendance, tardiness, truancy, student dress, off-campus policy, lunch, locks and lockers, school rules, suspension, hall passes, bus transportation, skateboarding, zero tolerance, school nurse, and cars at school; substitute teaching assignment by period; and the substitute time card.

First Things First

You will need some time to gather your thoughts before the students arrive. Use the lesson plans to write a short assignment on the board so that the students have something to do when they sit down. Write your name on the

Substitute Speaks...

For grades 4–12, put up on the board your name and these two phrases: I am glad to be here today. Please do not tell me that your teacher "always" lets you do something. AND please do not tell me that your teacher would "never" make you do something. Follow that with a BIG smiley face! Saves a lot of time! For lower grades, I love to greet the children in the hall and let them have a chance to hug me (and most of them do!). Every once in a while, smile mysteriously; they always wonder who you are getting ready to call on!

A lot of teachers have microwaves in their rooms. Sometimes on a Friday, I take a couple of bags of popcorn for the class (if they have behaved). It's an extra treat and they love it. Most of all: Relax and enjoy yourself. It will be fine and you love what you do, so you are sure to be good at it!

Miccilina M. Piraino
Full-time sub, grades K–12

board and the schedule for the day or the period as it appears in the lesson plan book or in the individual plans.

If you can't find an idea in the lesson plans, write down something for them to do for the first 5–10 minutes, if only a summary of what they read in the last chapter. Or direct the students to write three questions they have about yesterday's lesson. Or have a "quick write" or "quick draw" topic on the board for them to address. This should be done before the students arrive in the classroom or you pick them up at their designated lineup spot. Here are some examples:

1. What is your favorite book, movie, television show, music group?
2. What is your ideal career or profession?
3. What would be the best birthday gift?
4. List as many words as you can to describe your pet.
5. Use the word wall or your dictionary to write a story about your best friend.
6. Make a list of words that begin with_____.
7. What are the class rules and how would you change them?
8. Make a web of important information from your last chapter.
9. Do the crossword puzzle that is on your desk.
10. List all the sports you can think of.
11. Write an animal alphabet.
12. Name fruits you would put into a fruit salad.
13. Who is your hero?

14. Where in the world would you like to be right now?

15. How can you make a difference?

See many more ideas at this Web site:

(www.canteach.ca/elementary/prompts.html)

What to Look For

If your teacher has properly prepared for your subbing in his or her class-room, you should look for the sub folder, the lesson plan binder or folder, and possibly a tote or box of supplemental materials. Teachers themselves often leave a box or bag of motivating activities that they know their students enjoy. Experienced substitutes have learned to bring their own resources, but the ones provided by the teacher should be used first because they will be tailor made for the students, and your own supplemental materials, by necessity, will be generic.

Take some time to review plans before the students enter the classroom. The truly compulsive teacher will leave all the teaching materials you will need in a prominent place. The topic of interpreting lesson plans is covered in the next chapter.

Inferring Information from the Seating Arrangement

As you look around the room, even before the students arrive, you can glean a great deal of information from the way the seats are arranged. You can tell if there are study carrels for those who need to be isolated for one reason or another. You can tell what the teacher sees as his or her role by the positioning of the teacher's desk. Is it facing the students, letting them know that she or he is the one to look to, or is the desk in an unobtrusive spot, signaling, perhaps, that the teacher is in motion all day long?

When you find rows or modified rows oriented toward the front of the room, you can infer that the regular teacher is in charge and literally expects all eyes to be on him or her. It may also suggest that discipline issues may have necessitated the arrangement or that the regular teacher wanted to curb discipline problems at the outset. Many novices rely on seating to diminish talking and distractions. Row upon row of seats may convey the message that cooperative work is not the priority and that students work independently.

Clustered tables or desks suggest a social environment conducive to projects, cooperative learning, and differentiated learning. This configuration allows for sharing of materials and more interaction. The downside is that clustering may create management and even discipline problems for you. Make sure students at clustered tables can see you and the instructional focal points without turning into pretzels. This will make it more likely that they focus their attention on you when you ask for it.

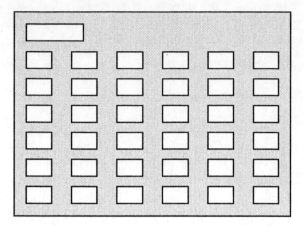

Figure 7.2   Rows

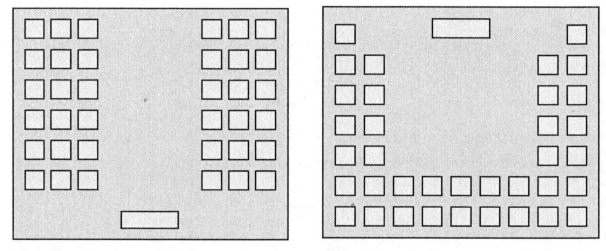

Figure 7.3   Rows Facing One Another   **Figure 7.4**   Horseshoe

The horseshoe configuration or seats facing one another, especially in middle and high school classes, suggests that the regular teacher encourages debate and discussions.

Look for isolated study carrels and be attentive to which students are seated at them.

Inferring Information from the Walls and Bulletin Boards

Instead of hearing about how things are done in the classroom, take a walk around the room with your eyes to see where storage cabinets are located, where the projection device is, where the screen is, where the computer stations are located, and so on. Look for a poster with rules and consequences, a point system, a token economy, and the like. Look for posters with directions, procedures, and instructions. Look for bathroom passes, hall passes, reward certificates, or treasure boxes of rewards.

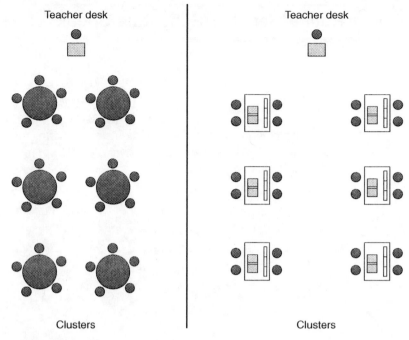

Figure 7.5 · Clusters

Figure 7.6   Classroom Rules

Starting the Day

The moment that the students enter the room, they will be sizing you up. This is the time to convey confidence and an energetic demeanor, one that conveys, "I am glad to be here and we will have a very productive day."

Stand at the door as students enter and tell them to take their seats. Tell them that you are subbing for their teacher and, if you know, let them know

Retired Teacher/Substitute Speaks...

If the students have been lined up, I have them stand quietly and then walk in and be seated and begin work on their first assignment or read for the few minutes while they are gathering. Then I write my name on the board in large letters and explain what it means and give a small introduction. It is important they know me as a person and as one who is there to assist them in learning and enjoying the day.

This introduction time lets me observe who listens, who might need extra attention. It lets me collect the clues that will guide our interactions. It is also the time to establish respect for one another. This helps avoid the rash of broken pencils and the urgent need to rush to the restroom. I try to use their names in positive ways and never at times of misconduct or mistakes. Mutual respect cuts out most discipline problems.

Betty Rosentrater

why she or he is absent. If you don't know why or when their real teacher will return, admit that as well. Ask them to work on the assignment until you turn the lights off as a signal for them to stop working.

Take some moments for yourself to scope out the students and their reactions to your being there. While the students are working, look over the plans again and prepare for the first learning activity. As you watch them working, you will also get a good idea of who starts to work right away, who dawdles, who looks confused, and so on.

Signal the students to stop and review what they have written or drawn. Repeat your name and emphasize that today will be a good day for learning. Allay anxieties about the teacher never coming back. Let them know that work will go on as usual. Explain that you are a pinch hitter who is here to save the day for learning in their teacher's absence. Use the seating chart to take attendance or have the teaching assistant in secondary schools take attendance on the computer. If you are confused about morning routines, ask the class who the leaders are and ask them.

Begin the class on time, as soon as the bell rings or as soon as the students are seated. This will help them understand that you are totally organized and know the ropes. While they are working on the assignment on the board, take attendance and make some notes for yourself, not only about absences but about those students who are tardy. Introduce yourself, tell something about who you are, and tell them what you know about when their teacher will return. They may already know that the teacher had a doctor's appointment or was attending a conference or inservice. Students can

Teacher Talks...

I don't leave a sub folder per se. I make a stack that is in order top-down from the beginning of the day to the end of the day. This would include any papers, including blank pages, that they might need so they don't have to go or look anywhere else. I leave the room number of a teacher who can answer questions for them or provide discipline help. I leave them a note on what I use for discipline, and my lesson plans would include any routines that I would have, including sending attendance to office, who says the pledge, recess duty, library, computer lab, and so on. I have this formatted in my home computer so when I need to write lesson plans it becomes paste and cut. I basically assume the sub knows nothing and I leave a script to follow.

Marsha Moyer
Third grade

Apply It!

The seating chart the teacher leaves can be a valuable assessment tool. Use the seating chart to monitor the students' in-class behavior and responses.

make their own nameplates by folding an index card in half. This will enable you to call students by name instead of having to refer time and again to the seating chart, if one is available at all. Spend just a short time on these preliminaries and get right to work.

Sample Elementary Schedule

This schedule is a template of common daily activities. The teacher you are subbing for may have a generic schedule in the sub folder. Before your first assignment, it is helpful to know what to expect for the day, including bell, recess, and lunch schedules and other special events you should anticipate.

Greetings. Welcome your students at the door and direct them to take a seat.

Routines/Morning Exercises/Flag

Classroom Rules Review

Language Arts/Reading. Distribute literature books, read aloud, or have the students write.

Recess/Snacks

Centers for Kindergarten or Math

Lunch

Science/Social Studies/Art

Wrap-up/Clean/Homework

Orderly lineup and dismissal

Generic Secondary Schedule

A buddy teacher in a nearby classroom will help you adjust the agenda since he or she knows about the bell and lunch schedules as well as other special happenings you should anticipate.

Greeting at the door

Administrative tasks

Goal for the period and class rules review

Preview the period

Activity as prescribed by the lesson plan

Wrap-up, cleanup, and homework assignment as prescribed by
the lesson plan

Orderly exit when *you* give the signal

Checklist for Your First Day of Subbing

✓ Arrive on time.

✓ Begin your day at the school office.

✓ Pick up materials that may have been left for you, including the key to the room, school map, bell schedule, lunch periods, special events of the day, and so on.

✓ Find out about the extra duties that you need to assume in the regular teacher's absence, including bus or playground duty.

✓ Look for a sub folder and supplemental resources in the classroom.

✓ Look for a lesson plan book or a set of lesson plans.

✓ Look around the room for clues as to rules, routines, seating arrangement.

✓ Write your name and the day's (period's) schedule on the board.

✓ Greet students at the door.

✓ Start the class or period promptly.

✓ Introduce yourself and tell them why you are there.

✓ Direct them to the assignment on the board.

✓ Take attendance.

✓ Go over the assignment on the board and start working from the teacher's plans.

✓ If none are available, use your own resources and contact the principal for further direction at the first break.

✓ Keep the students busy!

Avoid It!

Arriving late for your subbing assignment

Expecting a full set of plans and supplies to support instruction

Winging it in the class

Now that the students are present and accounted for, it's time to get down to business and begin the instructional period. Guidelines for interpreting the plans that have been left for you follow in the next chapter.

CHAPTER 8

Interpreting Lesson Plans

Effectiveness Essentials

- As a substitute teacher you are expected to follow the standards-based curriculum that is reflected in the teacher's plan book or lesson plans.

- If you are a long-term substitute, for as little as a week, become familiar with the standards and expectations of your district for the grade level or subject area.

- There are many variations on the lesson plan format.

- Seek help in deciphering lesson plans.

Of all the responsibilities of a new substitute teacher, none is more daunting (except perhaps classroom management) than interpreting the plans the teacher has left for you. They may be so detailed that any reasonable person could follow them, or they may be so skimpy that the holes in them resemble Swiss cheese. In this chapter you will learn about the rationale for following lesson plans, as opposed to winging it, and sample many variations on lesson plan formats. You will also learn that you will have to decipher some plans that may contain unfamiliar terms.

What Are Lesson Plans and Why Do I Need to Follow Them?

A lesson plan is a kind of thinking map that sets an end point and steps along the way to reach the goal. It is for you more than for the students because you want to help them get from here to there in an efficient way while enjoying the activities along the route. If you were traveling across the country by car to a friend's wedding, but didn't have a map, you might have quite an adventure wandering hither and yon. On the other hand, you might miss all the great sights along the way and the wedding as well!

Once you see enough lesson plans during your subbing experiences, you will notice they consist of three essential elements: objectives that derive from the standards, procedures, and evaluation.

1. Objectives that derive from the standards — Where do I want to go?
2. Procedures (including materials) — How will I get there?
3. Evaluation — How will I know when I arrive?

The lesson plans or plan book you will find on the teacher's desk should be based on the federal mandates of the No Child Left Behind Act, and it is incumbent on you to follow what is now a standards-driven curriculum.

The short time that you have to look at plans before you are on the hot seat will be easier if you understand where this standards-based movement derives from and how to prepare yourself beforehand to interpret those standards-based plans. Your time as a sub in the classroom, whether for a day or six months, must be based on more than your own teaching ideas and activities. You must incorporate the mandates of national, state, and local interests, as well as the needs of your individual students. In other words, you can't just "wing it" or do your own thing.

Standards-Based Plans and NCLB

Congress Declares...

On January 8, 2002, President George Bush signed into law the No Child Left Behind Act: "An act to close the achievement gap with accountability, flexibility, and choice, so that no child is left behind. Be it enacted by the Senate and House of Representatives of the United States of America in Congress assembled." U.S. Department of Education (2002)

No Child Left Behind has changed forever the way all educators look at curriculum, instruction, and assessment. NCLB establishes a system of state-mandated standards along with accountability to ensure that all students meet the standards, regardless of any mitigating factors, even having a substitute teacher. So NCLB affects you, too.

Under NCLB, states, districts, and schools that demonstrate improved achievement will be rewarded. On the other hand, schools that continually fail to meet set performance levels are sanctioned. Federal monies are now tied to performance. Parents and communities know how well their children are performing on annual state reading and math assessments, and schools are held accountable for their effectiveness. Read about specific provisions of NCLB at www.ed.gov/nclb/landing.jhtml.

The current administration has raised the stakes even higher by monetarily rewarding those states that adopt tougher standards and tie teacher and principal evaluation to student test scores. You can read about all the provisions of the initiative, "Race to the Top," at www.ed.gov/programs/racetothetop/index.html (2009).

Standards in the Grades or Subjects You Sub In

Become familiar with the standards and expectations of your district for the grade level or subject matter that you will encounter as a sub. If you have decided to specialize in one or two subjects or grade levels, your job will be easier. The Web site www.education-world.com/standards/ enables you to access standards by state or by subject matter for all subjects and grade levels. The schools and teachers you sub for are another source of the standards. And you should see the standards clearly marked on the lesson plans.

The more familiar you are with the overall curriculum, and especially the standards, the more comfortable you will be when you enter the classroom to sub. It won't take a long time, and you can keep a loose-leaf binder of the standards for the grades and subjects you are planning to sub in.

Teachers you sub for will follow these steps as they devise their plans. You are most likely only concerned with the last step if you are a day-to-day sub. If you are a long-term sub, or anticipate being one, all of the steps are relevant.

1. Know the curriculum and standards.
2. Divide it all among the school year so it all gets done.
3. Develop weekly plans.
4. Develop daily plans.

If you are subbing at the middle and/or high school level, standards can be interpreted more easily because you will only have one or two subject areas per assignment. The real challenge is dealing with the voluminous standards at the elementary level for each of the multiple subjects you instruct as a substitute teacher.

You may feel overwhelmed when you look at the curriculum materials and the lesson plans your teacher leaves for you. Some plans may not be clearly written in plain substitute teacher talk. How will you manage?

Look to Colleagues

The teachers at your grade level can help you interpret lesson plans or provide you with a copy of their lesson plans for the day. They probably know

Teacher Talks...

I have a piece of advice for teachers. Make sure you leave information for your subs about who is responsible and who needs to be watched because they are tricky. Do not assume that the sub knows all of the rules. I had a group of students that needed baby food jars or some form of container for a science project they were doing. The sub checked with other students and they pulled out their containers showing him that the four girls were telling the truth about needing containers. He did not check with the other teacher about particulars. He sent all four girls to the front desk to retrieve baby food jars. He should have checked with the other teacher first and he would have found that any type of container would work. He should also have sent only one student up. When they got back they convinced him that they needed to empty the jars and he said okay. They then pulled out spoons and proceeded to eat the food. If you know you have tricky students that should not be let out for any reason, make it clear in the sub plans so that things go smoothly.

Sandra Stiles
Sixth–Eighth Grade Reading Remediation

Teacher Talks...

Carefully read the teacher's plans for the day and special notes. Ask another teacher for help and make sure you know where things are; for example, the cafeteria, the office, and so on.

Be confident and let them know they are in good hands and everything is under control. I would review classroom procedures and rules with them to remind them of what is expected. You don't have to bribe them with candy.

Brandi Stephens
Fourth Grade

that their colleague left no plans if called away on an emergency, and if you ask them whether they have some plans to productively fill the day, they will be glad to help. If there are plans and you cannot figure them out, do not hesitate to ask colleagues what a certain acronym means or what they know about the strategies listed.

Look to Textbooks

The textbooks you find in the classroom will be a great help in providing you with information that you need to make the day go smoothly. You can ask the students to show you the last story they read, the last chapter they covered in a science text, the last math pages, and the like. Then you can

Resource Teacher Talks...

The hardest part about being a sub comes when you walk into a room with no lesson plans. It just ruins my day! I usually try to find last week's plans and see if I can figure out about where they are in each subject. The students are usually a great help in figuring out what lesson is next. Then of course comes the hunt for the Teacher's Edition. If I can't find the T.E., then I do my best in interpreting the student copy.

Starting with reading, I have the children reread the story they just finished. After rereading we talk about writing summaries (keep it short, beginning, middle, end, no details, only important events, etc.). Then I assign all students to write summaries of the story they just reread. As students finish their writing, they read what they wrote to the rest of the class as they are finishing their own work. Sometimes this helps the slow starter get ideas of what to write and how to make it sound good.

(continued)

(Continued)

During math time I try to assign something they have recently done. The challenge is for the capable students to get a perfect score and the others to see if they can use strategies they have already learned to calculate at least some of the correct answers. As students finish, they demonstrate how to find the answer to an assigned problem. In other words, the first one finished does number one, second one finished does number 2, and so on. Here again is a way procrastinators can check to see if they are doing the problems correctly.

For me the day usually ends here because the office has typically found a real substitute to finish the afternoon. As a resource teacher I advise that subs always come with a bag of lessons you love that are appropriate to the grade level you are teaching, If there are lesson plans use them, and be oh so happy the teacher went to all that work!

Linda Meyer

British Teacher and Sub ("Supply Teacher") Speaks…

I did a few months of substitute secondary teaching between jobs a few years ago. Bear in mind I had 19 years' teaching experience in everything from challenging inner city schools to elite, highly selective academic schools and boarding schools in the UK. The most important thing a supply teacher (sub) needs is high-quality material and information from the school or absent teachers about the lessons and classes, especially if you are only at the school for a day or so. Here is an anecdote that explains why.

I was an English teacher and I did supply at quite a tough school where in the morning I was given accurate, professional information and instructions for the variety of subject classes I was to teach. Everything went very well.

In the afternoon I had a class of 16-year-olds for math. The absent teacher had left me the sketchiest information, basically telling me what the pupils were to do from a textbook. When I started the lesson off, the pupils became difficult and disruptive, claiming that they had done the work before. When I examined a few exercise books, I found they were right. I tried to find some new work for them to do but it was almost impossible because I could not know what they did and didn't know.

Joe Nutt

Substitute Speaks...

When I get to a school and find that the teacher didn't leave lesson plans, the first thing I do is to see what they did the day before and continue the lesson. I look at the schedule and attempt to fill in so that the day can go smoothly. If there are no plans for the day before, I ask a teacher that teaches the same grade if I can make a copy of their plans and use that as my guide. The most important thing for me is to keep the children on the schedule that teacher has already set up.

Phyllis Guy

review the work and follow the advice of this resource teacher who is often called upon to sub while the secretary contacts a sub.

Lesson Plans in Many Formats

It is likely that from school to school and even from classroom to classroom, you will find that teachers have their own unique ways of laying out their plans and instructions.

Experienced teachers, who do not want to pick up the pieces after a chaotic sub day, will leave very complete and detailed plans in a format that is easily interpreted rather than long, detailed plans that may be required of them under normal circumstances.

The Elementary Overview Lesson Plan

Look at the sample in the boxed feature. This kind of lesson plan is written with the sub in mind. It provides time frames and specific pages in the Teacher's Edition as well as attaches sample assignments and notes about who will need extra help. But as well thought out as this plan is, you will notice the acronym DOL. If DOL (Daily Oral Language) is a mystery to you, ask a colleague. (It is an exercise in which students correct sentences with multiple errors.)

The High School Overview Plan

The same sort of overview lesson plan can be used in high school. The following overview for a high school special day class teacher enables the sub to see the big picture of how the day will go. Notice that the teacher is expressing gratitude and pointing the sub to the aide who can answer questions. Some subs may be hesitant to be assigned to special education classes, but I would urge you to accept these assignments so that you gain a window into the special needs of students who may not be so different from the ones you encounter in regular classes. If you are subbing to

CLASSROOM ARTIFACT

Grade 3

Good Morning,

Thank you for subbing for me.

****Thank you for following these plans as the students are used to learning a lot in one day. Please don't show any movies or give them free time or allow them to do their homework in class. Thank you for making sure the room is clean and all trash is picked up off the floor.****
Please feel free to use the camera projector if you know how.

8:50 Bell rings at 8:50 to let kids in classroom. Students work on Math-4-Today (have at their desk) last row. Give them 5–7 minutes, then go over answers. Caren collects homework and puts it on back table.

J. leads the class in the pledge. E. takes attendance to office.

9:05 Work on Problem of the Day (Thursday). Give them about 5–6 minutes, then go over correct answer with them.

9:10–10:30 Math

9:10–9:40 Review Chapter 4 with the students on page 70. Focus on problems 14–23.

9:40–10:20 Students take Chapter 4 test. Tell them to use scratch paper to solve problems. If they try to turn in a scratch paper without the problems worked out, hand the test back to them and tell them to work out the problems.

10:20–10:30 DOL (have at desk) Thursday of week 6

10:30–10:40 Recess no duty

10:40–12:05 Reading/L.A.

10:40– Vocabulary

With students, write a story using vocabulary words on page 131A in TE. Have students help you write a story by giving you sentences. Use poster chart in front of room to write on. Markers are on stereo stand.

11:00 Students will reread The Keeping Quilt with a partner to build read-aloud fluency. Those students who finish early, give them paper and have them make a list of common nouns in the story.

11:40 Whole Class—Read Nesting Dolls on pp. 154–157. Then have students fill out the Fact Finder Sheet.

12:05–12:45 Lunch—Walk kids to lunch line.

12:45–1:00 Teacher read-aloud. Pick a Patricia Polacco book off the board to read aloud to the kids while you dismiss them by table to get a drink. They get a 5-second drink and no talking is allowed.

1:00–1:20 Grammar

Quiz on common nouns; before you pass out the test ask students what a common noun is (a person, place, or thing that is not a name).

1:20–2:00 Writing—Students are to begin a draft of their personal narrative. Have them get out the graphic organizers they filled out yesterday. "Narrative

Voice," my sample, is attached. Tell students to take the information they have written down in their organizer and turn it into a story about themselves. They should be writing "Once I . . . Next I . . ." so the reader can tell it is a story about something that happened to them. Encourage them to describe rather than tell. Roger will probably need extra help in understanding what to do.

2:00–2:10 Recess, no duty

2:10–2:25 Teacher read-aloud. Pick a Patricia Polacco book off the board to read aloud to the kids while you dismiss them by table to get a drink. They get a 5-second drink and no talking is allowed.

2:25–2:50 Social Studies

Students are introduced to our new unit, Native American Communities, TE84. Follow TE on pages 84 & 85.

2:50–3:20 Science

Students are learning about the solar system. Follow TE on pages 232–233.

3:20–3:30

Have students get homework out of cubbies. Students pick up the floor and clean up desk area. All pencils, papers, erasers need to be put away. Review homework with students (assignments on the board).

3:30 Dismiss students.

Thank you

Marsha Moyer

CLASSROOM ARTIFACT

High School Special Day Class

Thanks for taking the position!

Wendy _____, my instructional assistant, should be in around 8:00 AM to help out! J_____, R_____, and J_____ can help you out with the rules and questions that you might have until Wendy arrives.

Period 1—math—All students are to have their folders and calculators on their desks and ready to work by the time the bell rings. Hand out page 6 sheet and give time for them to work on it or get started and then go over the sheet with them on the overhead or the whiteboard—use dry-erase markers on the whiteboard. T_____ has his own sheet, but may try p. 6 with a partner. Hand out puzzle exercise too for fun work.

Period 2—continue math if more time is needed. Hand out work sheet and give time for students to complete and walk around to assist as needed. Pair up students also—the kids can tell you who needs help and Wendy will help

(continued)

(Continued)

out with that too. Go over answers when most students are done and ask for volunteers to read their created sentences aloud. They usually enjoy that.☺ Please have J_____ or D_____ hand out homework and write student's name on them.

 Period 3—continue period 2 work if more time is needed. Have students pair up and read to each other in small 2–3 people groups according to their reading group of unit 15 or unit 36 for at least 15 minutes. They can tell you which group they are in. They should reread story until the 15 minutes is up. Read book "Don't Sit on My Lunch!" for fun.

 Period 4—Bingo. Write down the names of the winners and I will have prizes when I return.

 Period 5—conference.

 Period 6 Recreation class—They can play games, color, or look at magazines in groups or pairs.

Barbara Arient

decide if teaching is for you, you may decide, after working with students with special needs, that special education is where you belong!

 Also here is a lesson plan from a high school history teacher. In this plan you can see that the students will be doing group work using technology. They have been well prepared by the teacher and the sub will have an easy day of it.

CLASSROOM ARTIFACT

High School History Class

Sub Plans 3/20/09

US History Block 3

Japanese Internment Quick Presentations

1. Pass out booklets on Japanese Internment.
2. Read and complete the 8 questions for the reading of "Relocation of Japanese Americans." Students should also read the overview and background information. (give them 30 minutes to accomplish this task)

 They will turn in these answers for credit

3. Put into groups of 3 (there needs to be 6 groups) and provide one laptop computer per group. These computers are not to leave the room.

Each group will create a PowerPoint on the 6 topics of Japanese Internment

1. Immigration
2. Removal

3. Internment
4. Loyalty
5. Service
6. Justice

Students will use the Web page below to create a PowerPoint.

http://americanhistory.si.edu/perfectunion/experience/index.html

They can use a link to this Web page on the Grove Web site under my staff pages.

They can also use other sources.

They can make the PowerPoint on the school computer. Then save it to the Flash drive provided.

<u>Assignment:</u>
Create a PowerPoint that tells the story of the Japanese Interment Camps. Include:

1. The emotions, trials and real life experiences of the Japanese who were interned
2. Thorough coverage of the 6 topics with detail and accuracy
3. Pictures and quotes from your sources
4. At least 10 slides
5. Bibliography

Speech

The Generic Lesson Plan Format

You might find separate plans for each subject area, and these might include more information but without the time frames or specific insights into individual student needs. Many principals require lesson plans in the following format, and the teacher may not have simplified them for you. This generic plan format is required in some schools and in many teacher preparation programs. It has everything but the kitchen sink in it, but the completeness will help the sub when it comes to figuring out what to do.

The 5E Plan

There are several other formats you might encounter, depending on the subject matter and the grade level of the students. In science classes, you might encounter the 5E lesson plan (BSCS, 1997). This plan has a free exploratory phase followed by more structured input from the teacher. You will need to keep a lid on the enthusiasm of students working together in groups by

Generic Lesson Plan Format

Teacher_____ Subject_____ Time Requirements_____

Grade Level_____ Period_____ Date_____

Content Standards	List the standards that are being addressed in the lesson plan.
Prerequisites	This is the prior knowledge requisite for success.
Instructional Objectives	These derive from the standards and are tempered by the students' prior knowledge.
Adaptations	These are accommodations for English language learners and students with special needs, including the gifted.
Materials	All specialized equipment and materials are listed here.
Motivation	Description of how you will engage the students
Procedures	Steps in the lesson
Assessment/ Evaluation	Describes how you will determine the extent to which students have attained the instructional objectives
Follow-up Activities	Indications of how to reinforce and extend this lesson, including homework, assignments, and projects
Reflection	What went well, what adaptations should you make next time, what needs to be retaught as a result of the assessment?

CLASSROOM ARTIFACT

Grade 4 Integrated Lesson

This is a shortened version of a lesson plan developed by Elizabeth Hodgson, a K–5 science teacher, and Rachel Vogelpohl Meyen, a fourth-grade teacher, both from Durham, North Carolina, that follows the generic format. Notice that the acronym KWL may be unfamiliar to you, and so it is best to ask a student where the chart is located so you can figure it out yourself, or simply ask a student to tell you in his or her own words what a KWL chart is.

Topic: North Carolina History

Curriculum Areas: Social Studies, Language Arts, Computers/Internet

Grade Level: 4

Standards:

Social Studies

3.02—Identify people, symbols, events, and documents associated with North Carolina's history.

English Language Arts

4.02—Use oral and written language to present information and ideas in a clear, concise manner.

5.07—Use established criteria to edit for language conventions and format.

Technology

3.01 Create, format, save, and print a word-processed document.

Objective:

In pairs, students will work cooperatively to complete, edit, and publish a diary entry on the history of North Carolina.

Materials:

- Pencil
- Paper
- Computer w/ Microsoft Word software
- Tape recorder
- Blank tapes

Motivation:

Students have great latitude in choosing how they will present their information and the topic is directly related to where they live.

Adaptations:

English language learners are given dictionaries and are partnered with a native speaker to complete the diary entries.

Activities:

1. Diary Entry Writing (continued during the language arts period). This is a continuation of research they have done, and they should be able to complete their entries on their own and go on to #2, the next step, if there is time.
2. Publishing Diary Entries

Upon the completion of their writing, students should edit, save, and print (rewrite or retell) their entries, depending on their chosen medium.

Assessment:

Assessment of students' diary entry, using the *diary-writing rubric*. The students should complete their entries by the time the presentations are scheduled to begin even if they have not fully completed their editing process.

Follow Up:

KWL (Know, Want to Know, and Learned) Chart (Ogle, 1986)

Move the class's attention back to the original KWL chart. Add information to the "learned" column, and then begin a discussion and analysis of the misconceptions the students may have originally had about North Carolina's history of slavery and the Underground Railroad.

providing structure and clear directions, specifying time limits on exploration, and monitoring the group work.

Phase	Teacher Role
1 Engage	Motivate or capture the students' interest.
2 Explore	Enable the students to engage in a hands-on experience or experiment.
3 Explain	Introduce formal concepts and vocabulary.
4 Elaborate	Go into greater detail using the concept in different contexts.
5 Evaluate	Assess students' learning.

The Seven-Step Lesson Plan

Your teacher might prefer the popular seven-step lesson plan developed by Madeline Hunter. The phases are very similar to the generic lesson plan, but the steps have different names. This plan prescribes the following seven stages:

Phase	Teacher Role
Anticipatory Set	Motivates, focuses attention of students
Statement of Objectives	Tells students what they will accomplish
Instructional Input	Explains, lectures, demonstrates, gives instructions
Modeling	Demonstrates, shows
Check for Understanding	Watches faces, ask questions, asks for summary
Guided Practice	Guides and corrects students as they practice
Independent Practice	Monitors students as they work on their own

Helpful Tools to Understand Lesson Plans

When teachers write lesson plans or create assignments, they consider the level of thinking required of the students and the learning styles of students.

Bloom's Taxonomy

Teachers often use Bloom's Taxonomy (1964) as their well-established guide. The taxonomy consists of six hierarchical levels. In order to reach the higher levels, students often have to demonstrate their knowledge and comprehension of the materials before they can analyze, apply, synthesize, and evaluate. You will find a chart of Bloom's Taxonomy at the following Web site, and the levels are further explained, with examples, in Chapter 13.

www.nwlink.com/~donclark/hrd/bloom.html

Accommodating Learning Styles

Keep in mind that students generally learn best from hands-on, concrete experiences and that Gardner's (1993) theory of multiple intelligences implies accommodations to the learning styles of pupils. The teacher may have notations on the plans that describe which intelligences are being addressed. So here they are in a nutshell.

Intelligence	Strength	Examples
Linguistic	Sensitive to word meanings and order, verbal	Writers, playwrights
Logical-mathematical	Thinks abstractly, logical	Mathematicians
Spatial	Thinks in pictures, images, and metaphors	Architects, artists
Musical	Learns through musical patterns	Composers, dancers
Kinesthetic	Uses body and movement in learning	Athletes, dancers
Interpersonal	Understands others	Politicians, therapists
Intrapersonal	Operates in sync with emotions	Poets, novelists
Naturalistic	Uses the natural environment to learn	Environmentalists

Copy all the sub plans you are given and keep them in a binder. If you are assigned the same grade level or the same subjects to teach, you will have plans in your binder ready for some tweaking, but you won't have to start from scratch. Your subsequent subbing assignments will be easier because you already have some plans. Winging it is for the birds!

CHAPTER 9

Instructional Routines

Substitutes learn many routines by trial and error, common sense, or observation. One substitute reported "stumbling into what worked best." A *reliable* student can assist you by describing customary routines. You may be thinking that a tactical operations degree would be a useful supplement to your substitute preparation after reading about routines. In fact, logistics are a major factor in any complex endeavor, but especially in substitute teaching. Check to see whether the teacher has left you instructions regarding instructional routines. If so, you can follow these to the letter of the law. You can use a review of instructional procedures as a way of gleaning valuable information as well as a method of introducing yourself to the class. Ask some key questions such as: What do you do when you are finished with an assignment before the rest of the class? How do you signal that you need help? How do you label your assignments?

However, if you cannot find some directions, you will need to plan ahead for some instructional contingencies.

Effective Instructional Management

With a central tenet that *good discipline is dependent on effective instructional management,* Jacob Kounin (1977) developed a set of principles for instructional management. Here are Kounin's principles in a nutshell:

Ripple Effect occurs when a substitute corrects or praises one student and it influences other students to shape up or correct misbehaviors to earn the same praise. For example, when the sub says, "See how quietly Table 1 is waiting for instructions," all other tables come to attention with hands folded. Thanking secondary students for attention or readiness is appropriate and well received.

Withitness is defined as having eyes in back of your head or being aware of the entire class at all times. Before you begin, make sure all eyes are on you and keep scanning the room for potential disruptions. The students will want to test you to see if you are aware of what is going on. You can be sure there will be some monkey business until you prove your mettle by attending to deviations as soon as they occur.

Group Alerting means keeping everyone on task and making every class member accountable for responding. Using name cards or sticks is a great way of applying this concept. Look for a can of sticks or a deck of cards with student names on the teacher's desk. (See Figures 9.1, 9.2, and 9.3.) If you cannot find any devices to make calling on students fair and equal, you can make your own set of name cards. Buy a ring and attach cards after students write their names on them, or simply have them write their names on index cards. Before starting any lesson, you can follow the advice of this very experienced substitute teacher in order to keep the eyes on you and the group alerted for what is coming up.

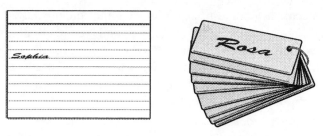

Figure 9.1   Ring with Small Index Cards and Index Card

Figure 9.2   Name Cards   **Figure 9.3**   Name Sticks

Retired Teacher/Substitute Speaks...

It is imperative first to gain the student's attention, then give all explanations clearly before moving on. By avoiding constant repetition, there is time left to actually help those needing help and spare the others from boredom. Varying the tone and volume of the voice and keeping it under control goes a long way toward holding attention. Silence often carries more weight than sound so I use it. Bursting into song can be interesting and exciting.

Another technique for gaining attention is to have something in hand. Having chalk or a marker ready to use causes students to anticipate something is likely to happen. When using the board, I like to use color to emphasize points. Size and position of words helps. Just to be sure we are all thinking of the same thing, I always keep a pointer on the ready. Moving about is another way to keep their attention. A hot, stuffy room slows students down so I snap on the lights, open a window for fresh air to revitalize them. I try to let them have physical ways to respond—raising their hands, clapping, tapping out patterns, and moving about in various ways . . . any controlled movement that ties into the lesson.

Betty Rosentrater

Satiation occurs as boredom sets in or when the students have had enough. Look for signs of restlessness, fidgeting, and a buzz of talking. It has been suggested that students can only attend to lessons for the same number of minutes as their age. That may or may not be true, but it is wise to structure a series of short lessons or allow for some breaks in between. You always want to leave your students asking for more.

Overlappingness is defined as the ability to attend to two activities at once—for example, walking over to a student who is playing with a toy, manipulating a handheld arcade game, or texting on a cell phone and confiscating the items without missing an instructional beat. A multi-tasking substitute teacher is essential in a busy classroom. Before you attend to outside business—for example, answering the classroom phone—assign an easy assignment such as, "Turn to the next page and read to summarize the content, paragraph by paragraph," or "Do the next three problems in your math text."

Pacing and Transitions should be smooth. Substitutes should be aware when lessons have gone on too long. Transitions between activities should be seamless and include closure and an introduction to what is coming next. You should follow these steps in order to efficiently move from one activity or lesson to another:

1. Have a student summarize the lesson.
2. Ask for questions.
3. Tell the students to put away the books/materials/supplies on their desk.
4. Have them take out books/materials/supplies for the next lesson.
5. State the objective.
6. Tell the students what they will be able to do as a result of learning the material.
7. Ask for questions.
8. Focus attention and begin.
9. Recycle from item 1.

Instructional Routines

The more you can routinize the procedures that support your instruction, the more smoothly the instructional period or day will go. The first place to look for instructional procedures is in the sub folder. Your next step should be to ask a *reliable* student how the teacher does *xyz*. You won't have to waste precious thinking time on all the mundane questions such as, "How will I collect papers today?" The more consideration you give to routines before you get to your subbing assignment, the more smoothly the day will flow.

Routines are only as effective as their constant reinforcement. So as you consider each and every routine that follows, apply these principles:

1. Begin as soon as you enter the classroom to reinforce any established procedures that will be in use during the day.
2. Be very specific as to how you want things done as per your teacher's instructions.
3. Have the students practice procedures, especially if you are making up your own or winging it without clear directions in the sub folder.
4. Liberally compliment students when they follow procedures.
5. Quickly deal with deviations from established procedures; for example, "I hear a good answer, but I won't call on anyone who doesn't raise his or her hand."

Help Needed

You need to establish a procedure for how your students can get help when you are busy. Teachers and subs find it frustrating to have elementary students tugging at their sleeves or reciting the mantra "Teacher, teacher" when they are involved during a small-group session. Secondary students will just sit there with raised hands or find more entertaining things to do when they are stuck and you are busy. Clearly explain the objective, encourage procedural questions, ask one student to repeat the directions, write all assignments on the board, identify alternative sources of help, and provide something meaningful for students to do when their work is completed. Create options such as these if there are no options posted on the wall:

- Ask the helper of the day.
- Ask a cross-age tutor.
- Ask one of the volunteer parents.
- Do what you can do and skip the hard parts.
- Use the word wall, instructional charts, spelling journal, dictionary, thesaurus.
- Whisper to a neighbor for help.
- Consult appendices in your text for formulas or conversions.
- Consult maps in your text.

Point to the *I Need Help* list when students come up to you. While this may sound extreme, you are actually establishing independence and making it more likely that students will either solve the problem themselves, learn to rely on peers for instruction, or discover the virtue of patience. If too many of your students are baffled, you need to reteach the material to the entire class or to a small ad hoc group.

If you are walking around the room encouraging questions, you certainly will get them. If you walk around repeating your already clear directions to individuals, you may be inviting learned helplessness. The subtle message is that there is no need to listen the first time. If you further allow students to come up to your desk whenever they want, they will use the wait line as a convenient way to avoid working.

Avoid It!

Don't encourage learned helplessness by jumping up every time you see a student who needs help. Provide clear directions, check for understanding, elicit questions, and then let them do some self-help before you intervene.

Controlling Noise

The best way to abate noise and chatter is to differentiate among whispering, talking, and silence. This is a useful distinction to make at the beginning of the day or period, because total silence is hard to maintain. You can make a game of this. Have students say their names with their voice and then whisper their names, using only their breath when initially calling on them.

Make some laminated circles to signal the appropriate noise level for the upcoming activity: green signifying talking, yellow for whispering, and red for silence. Specify the acceptable noise level for any one activity beforehand by pointing to or tacking the corresponding laminated color circle on the bulletin board. (See Figure 9.4.)

Teachers usually have a signal for total silence, like lights off, a bell, or a hand signal, and allow whispering at all other times. This information may or may not be in the sub folder, so be prepared with your own signaling device for silence.

One substitute puts a doll in a basket and announces that the baby is sleeping. Another cautions students not to awaken the rabbit (stuffed animal or real classroom pet). These techniques work well, even with older students, and you can have these props at the ready in your sub bag. Simpler devices for lowering the noise level are turning off the lights, playing music, or using a clapping pattern or nonverbal signal such as putting your finger to your lips. These tricks of the trade will remind students that the noise level has gotten too high.

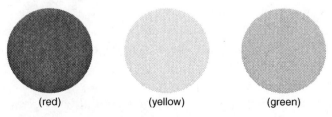

(red)   (yellow)   (green)

Figure 9.4   Noise Level Circles

Raising Hands

Be consistent about hand raising and avoid questions that elicit choral responses. Called-out responses or questions frustrate teachers and substitutes. Preface your questions with, "Raise your hand and tell us . . ." Always compliment and encourage students who remember to raise their hands, especially at the beginning of the day or period.

Free Time

To cut down on disruption when students finish quickly, you need to have some free-time ideas. Note that if the students are finishing too quickly, it may be evidence that the work is too easy or insufficient in volume. Bring a folder of activities, puzzles, crosswords, easy craft ideas, and the like. You can find additional suggestions in Chapter 15.

- Read a book.
- Play a game quietly.
- Take a puzzle and work it out.
- Work on some other unfinished project.
- Make up a crossword puzzle or acrostic.
- Work at the computer.
- Help others with their work or with learning English.
- Tidy up your desk.

Substitute Speaks...

I usually only sub elementary grades, but one time I worked at our local high school in a 10th-grade math class. They took a test for the first half of the class and then they were able to do whatever they wanted for the last half. Some talked, some studied, some even slept! This drove me crazy! I was so used to the "control" of elementary school. I ended up playing "Hangman" with the few who would give me the time of day.

Jane Stewart

Apply It!

What are some age- and subject-appropriate ideas for free time in the classrooms you are likely to sub in? Consider that most students love game formats, extra computer time, and creative curriculum applications. Jot down grade and subject specific ideas for later transfer to a file box or folder. Chapter 15 will give you a plethora of ideas for free-time fillers that are instructionally sound.

Labeling Papers

Schools, grade levels, departments, and teams often decide to have uniform labeling of papers. Check with a buddy teacher or *reliable* student to see what the norm is. But you will most likely need student name, date, subject, and, for secondary students, the period on each paper for easy identification when the papers get mixed up. Color-coding the papers by period is very useful if you have a long-term position and access to a variety of color papers at the copying machine. Use a different color copy paper for each period.

Collecting and Distributing Papers

You need to scan the room to see if there are student cubbies, folders, portfolios, or mailboxes for return of papers. Paper clip like papers together and apply a sticky note to identify the assignment. If you have time, alphabetize the papers. The teacher will love you when he or she returns.

Apply It!

Brainstorm all the other possible instructional routines you may need that have not been covered, given the subject or grade level of your probable subbing assignments.

Avoid It!

Don't change routines that are already established in the classroom. The students will be anxious enough that their teacher is absent, and you want to keep the day and its routines as normal as possible. If you cannot find the particular information in the sub folder, or from a *reliable* student, or from a buddy teacher, only then should you make an executive decision and create your own reasonable way of managing the situation. Tell the class that you will try to follow the regular classroom routine, but stress that to a certain extent, everyone does things somewhat differently.

In the next chapter you will find management routines, as differentiated from instructional routines. These are prerequisite to an efficiently run classroom and prevent many of the *discipline* problems that subs so fear.

CHAPTER 10

Essential Routines for Classroom Order

Effectiveness Essentials

- Routines provide the safety and security students need, especially in the teacher's absence.

- Identify all routines from the sub folder, a buddy teacher, or a *reliable* student.

- Allow the students to be helpful in terms of explaining or clarifying procedures.

- Use established routines for exits and entrances and other purposeful out-of-seat activities such as pencil sharpening, bathroom, water fountain, and moving to groups.

Routines in the classroom will enable you to provide the stability, safety, and security the students need, especially since their teacher is absent and they may be concerned, confused, and anxious. Don't reinvent the wheel unless you are a long-term sub. The more stability in the classroom, the less likely it is that disruptions will occur. If regular, well-practiced routines are maintained by you, the effort spared can be used for more stimulating instructional activities that will make your day or period fun for both you and the students.

Routines create order, and when the basic operation of the classroom is under control, you and the students will feel less stressed. In this chapter the emphasis is on trying to keep the routines as normal as possible and following the guidelines provided by the teacher.

Apply It!

As you read the following third-grade classroom artifact written for substitute teachers by a very organized teacher, you will probably notice that not all the routines you may need are covered. Very often teachers embed the routines in the lesson plan, and you have to be a very good detective to find them. Make a list of routines that are covered in this artifact and then make a list of questions that arise, such as: How do I distribute the homework papers? Are they allowed to use the bathroom? How about lining up?

CLASSROOM ARTIFACT

Grade 3

Sub Plans for Thursday, January 24, 2008
Duty-None

7:50-9:10   Pick students up on playground. Take roll, lunch count, and do flag. C. will hang roll up on door for you. Collect their homework.

Please have the students do board work. Turn on the Elmo. A. will know how if you don't. They are to correct sentences 5 & 6. Please show them how to do workbook pages. (You can put the workbook on the Elmo and show them how to do the pages.) They are to complete all activities on the board. They know how to do these as they do them daily. They should be done at about 9:00. Use the cards and call on them to correct their work. Have someone read journal. They get tickets for correct answers.

9:10-9:25   Recess. (If it is a rainy day they must stay inside. Excuse them by table to go to the bathroom and you may play heads up 7-up or silent ball.) If you need a break call 501 and ask them if someone can come to give you a bathroom break.

9:25-9:55   Finish up correcting if you are not done. Have mayors pass out paper for spelling and vocabulary test. Number from 1–16. Words are on TE 43F. Have them turn over for vocabulary. They need to do these words on the back of their paper: Creek, calf, bilingual. They may draw a picture or write the definition or both. They know the routine.

9:55-10:20- Read with them "I Work in the Ocean," pp. 66–69. Discuss.

10:20- 11:10   Read Aloud- Read to them about Dr. Martin Luther King and discuss. Have them do packets.

11:10-11:45-   Lunch. Send them out to recess first. If it is a rainy day walk them up to cafeteria in alphabetical order.

11:45-12:05-   Pick them up on playground. If it is a rainy day pick them up in the cafeteria. They have Dear time (Silent Reading). Table 5 may go to the library.

12:05-1:05-   Math. Mad Minutes (turn on timer for 1 minute). Have C. stamp papers. If they finish they get a sticker. Have them do the test for Math 4 today. They have this at their desk. It is #26. Then you may play multiplication bingo with them. The winner may go to my treasure chest.

1:05-1:15   Recess (If rainy day keep them in)

1:15-1:35-   Awards Assembly - Take them to cafeteria. Give the awards to whoever is in charge and they will pass them out.

1:35-1:55-   I will leave you a science movie to watch.

1:55-2:00-   Clean up. Give out table points to the 2 cleanest tables. Walk them out to the front of school.

Please leave me a note as to what you completed and how class behaved.

> Thanks
> Diane Amendt

---

*Note that an ELMO is a digital projection device.

In the worst-case scenario there will be holes in the instructions you receive from your teacher in the sub folder or on the lesson plans regarding the routines that stave off chaos. And the *reliable* student turns out to not be as reliable as you were led to believe. And you don't want to ask the entire class about logistics because the chorus of 35 "advisors" will respond with a cacophony of diverse responses. Compounding this worst-case scenario, there are no colleagues you can turn to and the buddy teacher next door is too busy to provide much guidance. You are on your own. This perfect storm of a total information blackout will never happen, but just in case . . . in this chapter you will learn how to implement some simple routines if need be. These include routines for:

- Entering and exiting the classroom
- Materials and supplies
- Bathroom and water fountain
- Movement within the room

Entrances and Exits

The way in which students enter the room sets the tone for how the day or period will go. Have your elementary students form lines outside the classroom prior to entering. While school rules may be more relaxed, lines diminish pushing and shoving and discourage barreling into the room.

Lines also help to make a smooth transition from socializing outside to work in the classroom. These same procedures can be followed during any entrance into the room, whether from recess, physical education, or from another part of the building.

Lines are most readily enforced in elementary school. In middle and high schools, use entrance and exit routines that are customary, but be sure the students enter the room ready to learn. Meet the students at the door where you can more easily monitor them and ensure an orderly entrance. Every moment counts in a short period. You don't want to waste half the period quieting rowdy students, and one way of avoiding this is insisting on an orderly entrance. Meeting the students at the door also helps you establish your presence, and you can greet them with, "Good morning. I will introduce myself and explain why I am here when you are all seated."

Establish a procedure for what you expect the students to do when they enter the room. Turn off all lights when you leave the room and establish the turning on of the lights as a signal that the next activity is about to begin. Or, better yet, have an activity on the desks or on the board for the students to do as soon as they enter the room in the morning or after breaks. Some teachers have students write in their journals first thing in the morning and read their books first thing after lunch.

The third-grade classroom artifact has very clear instructions for what the students do upon entering the classroom; that is, board work. Look for the initial activity on the lesson plans before the students even arrive. Write the directions on the board and instruct them to get to work.

Similarly, in middle and high school, write a short assignment on the board for students to complete at the outset. If the teacher hasn't left a short assignment, design one on the spot. In a history class, for example, "Which

historical event would you have liked to witness first hand, and why?" In an English class, "Who is your favorite character in the book so far, and why?"

These alternatives will give you a few minutes to collect your thoughts, especially in the morning and after lunch when clerical tasks may command your attention and you need time to review the period's or day's plans and other important items in the sub folder.

Apply It!

What can you have the students do in the first few minutes of school or the first few minutes of the period? This should be an assignment that has both a management and an instructional purpose. Prepare a list of ideas for the grades and/or subjects in which you are likely to sub. Chapter 15 has a very comprehensive list of ideas.

In elementary school dismiss by table or row with the quietest table leading the pack. Combining the group dismissal with the line is another alternative. By table, students line up for P.E., recess, lunch, library, assembly, or final dismissal. You can dismiss by some clothing attribute: students wearing stripes or red tops, white tennis shoes, or a sweater, for example. This is not only a good way to have students line up for dismissal, it provides a nonthreatening way to teach basic concepts to English language learners in early grades.

When moving around the school with elementary students, walk in the middle, not at the front. When you lead the line, the students at the back of the line will create their own party. When you bring up the rear, the students in the front will get away from you. Give clear directions about stopping points along the way. For example, "Stop at the water fountain," or "Stop in front of the office and wait for me."

In secondary classrooms, you don't have the luxury of a slow dismissal because it is essential that students get to their next class on time. You need to establish a quick method like dismissing by those rows or tables that are packed up and ready to go. But be sure to let them know that you will give the signal for dismissal when everyone is packed up, *not* the bell.

Transitions are unstable times in a classroom. No matter what the grade level, the more structure you give to the situation, the more likely it is that safety and low noise level will prevail. This is true especially when the exit from the room is required for simulated (or real) emergencies such as fire drills. In large gatherings, such as assemblies or rallies in high school, there is usually an established order of dismissal. Find out what it is and take note.

The sub folder should have directions regarding fire drills, earthquake drills, and other simulated, potential, or real emergencies. It is essential that you read all the emergency-related information in the sub folder. If there is a real emergency, *you* are responsible for getting everyone out safely and quickly.

Materials and Equipment

Schools are not yet paperless environments. There is much teacher "stuff" in classrooms that needs to be accessed, monitored, distributed, and collected efficiently. Student "stuff" in desks, in cubbies, on hooks, or in lockers presents yet another organizational challenge.

Ascertain what materials may be accessed by students by asking that *reliable* student. The teacher's desk and file cabinet or special supply shelf is usually off limits to the students. Similarly, their cubbies, desks, and coat hook are off limits to you. The teacher you are subbing for probably will not explain materials distribution/collection to this level of specificity, so you need to ask a student or decide yourself whether students will be allowed, for example, to get whatever papers they need when they need them, or will monitors hand out papers, or will you pass the papers out yourself to individuals or to monitors? Will monitors collect papers, or will you collect them? Do you see a central collection tray labeled as such? How will students get pencils, crayons, scissors, and paste? Are these items on the desks or at a central location? When in doubt, choose structure.

Bathroom and Water Fountain

You do not want the students to miss valuable instruction, especially in light of two recesses and lunch break in elementary school and time between periods in secondary school. Check the teacher's plans or other informational documents to see if a bathroom policy is included. Students will tell you all sorts of rules for using the bathroom in the event the teacher hasn't left any guidelines for bathroom use. Before creating your own rules about bathroom usage during class time, ask colleagues or department heads what the school norms are. You do not want to deviate from them. In kindergarten look for signs of imminent bathroom need.

Look for bathroom passes hanging in the classroom. Most teachers use a pass system. The passes will clue you in to when students are allowed to leave the classroom for bathroom breaks. In any event, you can add these rules:

- Do not leave during instructional time or when directions are being given.
- Wait until a pass is available.
- Keep all restrooms neat and tidy for others.
- Leave and return without disturbing others.

   1. Teach the students to use American Sign Language to signal that they need to use the restroom. The sign is the one for the letter T. Make a fist and

Figure 10.1   Bathroom Passes

Figure 10.2   ASL Sign for Toilet

insert thumb between the index and middle finger and move it side to side. This will be a silent signal that will not disturb others. (See Figure 10.2.)

2. Require students to leave a placeholder on their desks when they need to use the restroom. This lets you know who is out of the room, especially in large classes where a visual reminder may be needed. (See Figure 10.3.) You can add these laminated placeholders to your sub bag, especially if you sub in high school.

Water access is not as necessary as bathroom breaks. Water is always available at recess and at passing times. When fountains are in the room, you may choose to allow students to drink, as they require liquid nourishment, but beware! Since there is a direct connection between drinking and bathroom requests, you may be simply adding to management problems if you provide access to water all day, even within the room. In high school,

Figure 10.3   Placards to Put on Table When Student Leaves Room

depending on the rules, students carry big, bulky water bottles and drink from them all period long. You can make a water rule that allows one water break during class on very hot days. Since the periods are so short, you are not committing the misdemeanor of student dehydration or water deprivation. They can drink before and after class.

Movement Within the Room

Your students, especially the energetic ones in elementary school, need teacher-sanctioned opportunities to stretch and amble. Secondary students move about between classes, but the elementary students need to move about periodically, too.

Structured Movement

You can structure periodic in-class exercise routines. There are several excellent DVDs and CDs that feature classroom-appropriate controlled exercise routines. Add these to your sub supplies. When you provide the opportunity for exercise, fewer students are likely to make their own individual opportunities that can disrupt and cause delays. In the upper grades or middle school, after establishing a signal for returning to work, you may want to schedule periodic five-minute mini-breaks to enable this peer-dependent group to socialize.

Managing Pencil Sharpening

The constant grinding noise of a sharpener can grate on the ears and disrupt instruction. Many teachers use a pencil exchange, so look for a can of sharpened pencils in the room. Be prepared and bring some pencils with you that are distinctive so you can get them back at the end of the period or day. Then there is no need for students to get up and move around to sharpen pencils.

Access to the Wastebasket

You can't eliminate totally the need to get rid of dirty tissues or paper scraps. Assign a monitor to pass the basket during transition times.

Moving to Groups

If the elementary classroom is typical, you will notice charts/visual aids for moving to groups for small group instruction or for moving to centers. Look around the room for clues as to how students rotate to groups if you can't locate information in the sub folder. To ease transitions from groups to seat work to activity, teachers generally make two charts, one listing the names of all members of each group and another that signals what activity each group is engaged in. A wheel arrangement or pocket chart are standard. So look for these management devices.

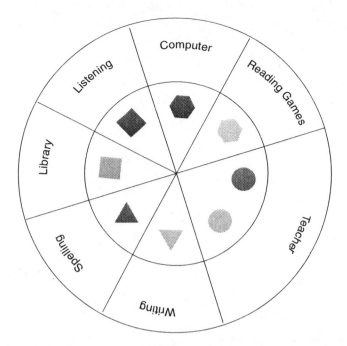
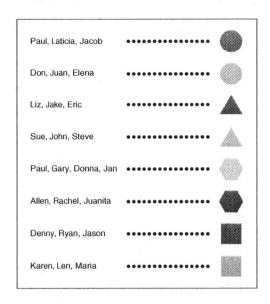

Figure 10.4 Center Rotation Wheel and Group Names

***

Avoid It!

Don't reinvent the wheel. Stick with established routines.

Create *very simple* routines if need be.

Have a response ready for, "Mrs.___ doesn't do it that way."

***

CHAPTER 11

Clues to Classroom Discipline

Effectiveness Essentials

- Look for the classroom rules and review them with the students.
- Look for clues to the teacher's discipline system in the room.
- Rely on the teacher's system.
- Be positive rather than punitive.

Most substitute teachers are concerned about classroom discipline and what to do when the students engage in negative behaviors. This is not altogether an unrealistic concern, because traditionally students see the substitute teacher as powerless.

Retired Teacher/Substitute Speaks...

The hardest thing about subbing, hands down, is having to discipline students with someone else's discipline policy, especially if it is something that doesn't work for you. Every teacher has a discipline policy that's comfortable for him or her but won't always work for someone else. I always find myself having to compromise.

Sally Steinbrunn

Looking for Guidance in the Sub Folder

First, take a good look at the materials you find in a sub folder and try to discern what the discipline plan might be. If you are fortunate, you might find in your plans a note such as this one, which details how rewards are earned.

CLASSROOM ARTIFACT

Grade 3

Rewards

I run my class with rewards.

Tickets: They get tickets for an individual reward. They get them for answering questions correctly or any other individual thing that they might do. They use them for pencil sharpening, drinks of water, going to the bathroom. They may purchase a pencil or eraser with their tickets. They may use them on Friday for the treasure chest.

Table Points: You may give these out for table groups who are quietly working, or tables that come in and sit down quietly. You may give them to the table that is ready to go first. At the end of the day they are given to the cleanest 2 tables.

Party Points: These are for the whole class. Please give them out if the whole class does a good job in assembly, library, or on the day that you sub.

Diane Amendt

Look for Classroom Rules

Next, take a look around the room for the list of classroom rules. These are the rules that the teacher expects you to enforce with the students. Review the rules before starting any instructional activities. Rules come in a variety of formats, but generally you will find them posted on a bulletin board, written on a large poster, or written in high school students' notebooks.

In elementary school, common rules are:

1. Respect property and rights of others.
2. Follow directions.
3. Be a good listener.
4. Raise your hand to speak or leave your seat.
5. Work quietly.
6. Do your best.

Sometimes you may find a "Classroom Constitution" signed by all students who agree to:

1. Listen and follow directions.
2. Raise our hands to speak.
3. Work without disturbing others.
4. Be responsible.
5. Be kind to others.

At the middle and high school levels you may encounter rules such as these:

1. Obey all school rules.
2. Be in your seat when the bell rings.
3. Bring all required materials (including homework) to class.
4. Raise your hand to speak and be a good listener.
5. Be respectful and responsible.
6. Come to class prepared to work.
7. Plagiarism and cheating result in failure.

Enforcing Rules

Be consistent in enforcing the rules. Students will be waiting to see what you do when a rule is broken. A good strategy when someone breaks a rule is to ask that student to hold up the number of fingers that represents the rule that needs to be followed. This will let the other students know that although you are not the regular teacher, you know the rules and will apply them.

On the odd chance that you cannot find the rules posted somewhere in the room or in the materials the teacher has provided, ask a neighboring teacher or ask the designated student helper/teaching assistant. If no one has

Teacher Talks...

You set the tone for the class. You are the teacher, not a friend or "fake" teacher. You are a professional, so present yourself that way. Always let the class know what you expect, the consequences (good and bad), and stick with them. All children will push boundaries. Being a teacher means that they will not always like you; however, it is your responsibility to have them respect you. In every one of my classes I've always established respect, clear rules, clear boundaries, and clear consequences FIRST. Have fun with them and enjoy your time substituting!

Sidney Gaskins

been so designated, take a chance and call someone who "looks reliable" or the class president/leader up to your desk and ask him or her where you can find the classroom rules or what the classroom rules are.

If there are no classroom rules at all (and that would be highly unusual), use any of the rules listed above as your guide and present them to the students as your special substitute rules.

Teacher Talks...

The most important advice that I like to give subs is to be firm and establish your rules from the beginning of the day and then consistently reinforce them.

David Emrick
Fifth grade

Thank all the students who are adhering to the rules by giving out copious compliments such as, "Thank you for following Rule # __ ," or "I am happy that you are all remembering to raise your hands." If a rule is broken, but not intentionally, say something like, "I hear a terrific answer, but Rule # ___ requires that your raise your hand." You will gain much more respect if you deal with rule breakers kindly with language such as this.

Think about your bottom line with rules. If you try to deal with every little infraction, there will be no time for teaching. You can ignore some minor violations or simply say, "I am letting that go this time because everyone makes mistakes."

Retired Teacher Talks...

Discipline and Substitutes

When the teacher doesn't leave a discipline routine for the class you have to come up with something, quickly. Try to be positive, remember the goal for everyone is to get through the day smoothly. I asked my daughter, Stephanie, who teaches 6th grade in middle school what she does. She said, "I quickly come up with my own set of rules and take enough time so I know the kids really understand them".

Consequences need to be appropriate for the grade level. Hopefully after warnings, a few minutes late to recess, removing the student from a "fun" or class-involved activity, there won't be too many problems.

Remember, generally positive rewards . . . table points or stars which lead to the one minute early to recess, or first in line for lunch, etc. really work.

Try not to fall into the "Names on the Board" trap. You can be assured that the teacher knows which students will misbehave. Also, don't tattle on recess problems; the playground aides will inform the teacher of any serious infractions. One time I returned from an absence with 20 names on the board, and a note from the substitute informing me that my class was the worst she had ever seen. So when the students came in, I let them vent 5 minutes verbally about all of their perceived injustices. Then they wrote for 10 minutes, after which I collected the notes (to put in the round file) and told them I would read each one of them. Obviously, I did not have that substitute again.

Shirley Clark

Identifying Discipline Systems

As you look around the room, it may not be that easy to discern the teacher's overall system of discipline because rules are common in all systems. You will need to see the big picture that goes beyond a list of rules. Here are the basic plans in a nutshell.

Behavior Modification

In behavior modification systems rewards and penalties are assessed by teachers to modify behavior extrinsically. After the rules are handed down (or, in some instances, established with students) and then practiced, an intricate system of rewards and penalties is initiated. Canter's work in assertive discipline (Canter & Canter, 2001) and Jones's work (1992, 2000) are examples of systems based on rewards and penalties. One reward Jones suggests is Preferred Activity Time (P.A.T.), in which teachers use a stopwatch to either subtract or add free-time minutes. If students take away teaching minutes through misbehavior or inattention, then they are docked free-time minutes. Some of the other positive rewards that teachers use for appropriate behavior are the following:

Elementary

Individual	**Whole Class**
Certificates	Popcorn parties
Special activities	Field trip
Stickers, small gifts	Extra P.E. time
Candy	Ice cream party
Homework exemption	Special activity
Verbal praise	Verbal praise
Honor Roll	Preferred Activity Time (Jones)

Middle and High School

Individual	**Whole Class**
Computer time	Activities the students enjoy
Recognition certificates	Free time
Fast-food coupons	
Homework passes	
Gel pens, key chains	
Posters	

In some classrooms, you may find a token economy in place. Students earn tickets (raffle type available at office supply stores in rolls) for positive on-task behaviors. They write their names on the tickets, and at the end of the week a drawing is held. Those whose names are drawn get to go to the treasure chest that contains a variety of items to choose from. The small and inexpensive items are greatly valued by the students, and the system works very effectively, especially because tickets are given to students who are "caught doing the right thing."

Rewards can be earned individually, in groups, or as a whole class. Teachers make a chart of students' names and use stars, move pushpins, or color in the spaces when students earn points. If the record keeping is done for groups at a table, the entire table is listed and points accrue when all the students at the table are doing the right thing. Some teachers run the system by total class and add marbles or popcorn kernels to a jar when everyone is behaving appropriately. A full jar means a popcorn party or special treat. Some teachers announce the number of points or marbles to be earned before each activity begins.

These incentive programs take special effort, and as a sub, you must be consistent and fair in using them. Students will clamor for points and keep

you on your toes if you forget. If the regular teacher uses these systems, it will be up to you to continue with them, even though the management of these systems may cause more disruption in your class than the behaviors they were designed to correct in the first place.

On the flip side of the rewards system are the various penalties that teachers assess for infractions of the rules. When this happens, depending on the system, students gather negative checks on the board, on a teacher's clipboard, or on a color-coded chart that translates into increasingly negative

Retired Teacher/Substitute Speaks...

Have a "carrot" you can dangle that they can look forward to IF THEY BEHAVE. I like to play Bingo with them at the end of the day with simple prizes for the winners. Even promising to read a favorite book at the end of the day can be a motivation for younger students. Older kids always want to play P.E. so you can promise to extend their P.E. time. Have some kind of warning signal to let them know how they are doing throughout the day. I start to draw a stop sign on the whiteboard. The students know that if I complete the stop sign, they will not get the reward. However, I will also erase part of the stop sign during the day if I see improvement in behavior.

Sally Steinbrunn

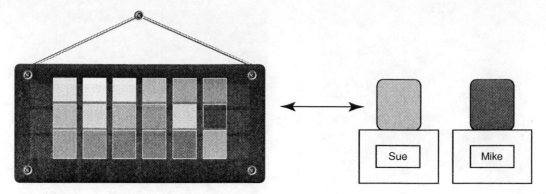

Figure 11.1   Pocket Chart with Color-Coded Cards

consequences. These may include staying in for recess, staying after school, going to the principal's office, carrying a note home, or missing favorite activities.

Many secondary schools use a referral process. Penalties in middle and high school may include detention, isolation, fines, and suspension, combined with parental notification. You will be expected to follow the referral procedures and be in line with the other staff members in identifying those behaviors that mandate suspension as punishment.

In middle and high school, since you only see the "culprit" for one or two periods, it is hard to follow up. Before you encounter your first severe behavior problem, find out what the policy is for serious infractions in your middle or high school and the steps you must take.

Encouragement and Logical Consequences

Encouragement is offered by Dreikurs and others (Dreikurs, Grunwald, & Pepper, 1998) as an alternative to praise. Encouragement means that you don't have to be 100% perfect. It means you have made progress along the way and that progress is noted and supported. Encouragement gives you the will to continue on the right path. Praise suggests completion, approval for a job well done or an achievement.

All students, and especially the discouraged ones, need opportunities to experience success. Encouraging the small steps on the way to success is as important as completion of the whole task. If a misbehaving student is a discouraged student, as Dreikurs and colleagues (1998) assert, then your goal as a sub is not to give false praise that the students know is not deserved, but rather to help students achieve small victories by encouraging them. Some ways of encouraging students include:

Recognizing effort as opposed to success
Pointing out helpful contributions
Highlighting the improvements you observe

Assigning special jobs that the student can succeed in

Asking the student to assist others who need help

Displaying the student's work

Demonstrating in word and deed that you believe in him or her

Your encouraging words might include:

Don't give up. I know you can figure it out.

You have improved in . . .

Let's try it together.

You do a good job of . . .

You can help me by . . .

I'm sure you can straighten this out.

Apply It!

Encouraging statements build upon strengths and minimize errors. Encouraging statements focus on the intermediate steps, not the end result. Identify the following statements as either encouragement or praise. If they are praise statements, turn them into encouragement:

1. You have taken a good deal of care with your handwriting. Together let's work harder on your spelling. P/E

2. That's a difficult question, but I am sure you will figure out the answer. I'll give you a hint. P/E

3. You are the smartest science student I ever had. P/E

4. You are a terrific athlete. P/E

5. Your help giving out the papers was much appreciated. P/E

6. Today you remembered to raise your hand to answer questions most of the time. P/E

7. You are the greatest helper in the class. P/E

8. You worked quietly during language arts time today. P/E

9. Take another look at your computation to find a small error. P/E

10. Super duper job on that! P/E

(Answers: Encouragement 1, 2, 5, 6, 8, 9; Praise 3, 4, 7, 10)

Just as encouragement is an alternative to praise, logical consequences are an alternative to punishment. While punishment is applied solely by the teacher and may be generic (miss recess, call to parent, visit to principal or dean), in the logical consequences approach, the student experiences the natural or logical consequences of his or her own behavior and the consequence is not generic.

Logical consequences are always related to the offense, reasonable, and respectful. A student who writes on the desk cleans it up during recess.

A student who fights on the playground sits on the bench for a day or two. A student who spills the paint mops it up. Students are usually given the choice between stopping the misbehavior or accepting the logical consequence. Logical consequences are never humiliating, and they teach students about responsibility and the relationship between actions and consequences. Remember to use the phrase "make a better choice" before you try anything else.

Beyond the Discipline Systems: Very Serious Infractions

The most serious, unlawful offenses need to be dealt with swiftly according to your district's policy, which derives from your state education code or laws governing education.

Students in middle and high school may take their offenses to an even higher level. Behaviors that should concern you include fighting, name-calling, stealing, cheating, plagiarism, destruction of property, constant defiance, bullying, refusal to work, profane language, and threats of violence, among others. There are no tried-and-true recipes for dealing with these behaviors, but certain general principles apply.

Except when students are in danger, it is best to deal with serious infractions when you are calmer and better able to act in a rational manner.

Keep detailed records (anecdotal) of the student's behavior with the date, descriptions of the behavior, and your response. Detailed anecdotal records will be helpful to the teacher when he or she returns to school.

CLASSROOM ARTIFACT

Excerpts from the California Education Code with Reasons for Suspensions from A-Q 48900

A pupil may not be suspended from school or recommended for expulsion, unless the superintendent or the principal of the school in which the pupil is enrolled determines that the pupil has committed an act as defined pursuant to any of subdivisions (a) to (q), inclusive:

(a). 1. Caused, attempted to cause, or threatened to cause physical injury to another person.
   2. Willfully used force or violence upon the person of another, except in self-defense.
(b). Possessed, sold, or otherwise furnished any firearm, knife, explosive, or other dangerous object. . . .
(c). Unlawfully possessed, used, sold, or otherwise furnished, or been under the influence of, any controlled substance. . . .

(d). Unlawfully offered, arranged, or negotiated to sell any controlled substance. . . .

(e). Committed or attempted to commit robbery or extortion.

(f). Caused or attempted to cause damage to school property or private property.

(g). Stolen or attempted to steal school property or private property.

(h). Possessed or used tobacco, or any products containing tobacco or nicotine products. . . .

(i). Committed an obscene act or engaged in habitual profanity or vulgarity.

(j). Unlawfully possessed or unlawfully offered, arranged, or negotiated to sell any drug paraphernalia. . . .

(k). Disrupted school activities or otherwise willfully defied the valid authority of supervisors, teachers, administrators, school officials, or other school personnel engaged in the performance of their duties.

(l). Knowingly received stolen school property or private property.

(m). Possessed an imitation firearm.

(n). Committed or attempted to commit a sexual assault. . . .

(o). Harassed, threatened, or intimidated a pupil who is a complaining witness or a witness in a school disciplinary proceeding. . . .

(p). Unlawfully offered, arranged to sell, negotiated to sell, or sold the prescription drug Soma.

(q). Engaged in, or attempted to engage in, hazing. . . .

Source: California Department of Education. (2008). Education Code. [Online] www.cde.ca.gov. Retrieved November 19, 2009.

In California, a student can be suspended for infractions that seem unimaginable and unlikely, but they happen. You will have to call the office immediately if one of these very serious infractions occurs.

Once you understand the basic systems, you will begin to notice clues around the room that will help you discern which system(s) are in place. You need not fear that there will be a total lack of information. If there is, just create your own rules.

Remaining Positive in Any Discipline System

Whatever the system, certain principles will help you have a great day and enjoy the students. Marzano and colleagues (Marzano, Marzano, & Pickering, 2003) suggest that conveying a positive and enthusiastic attitude with students will alleviate many behavior problems. That means teachers should have equal parts dominance (leading and controlling the class) and cooperation (willingness to take a personal interest in students and in the class as a whole). Here are some ways to create a positive classroom climate and model respect for the students. Aspire to rate high on the fairness quotient.

1. Treat everyone as equally as you can.
2. Deal with confrontations privately.
3. Respect students' private spaces.
4. Show respect for all students and value diversity.
5. Give the student(s) an opportunity to make things right before you resort to punishment.
6. Smile when appropriate.
7. Move around the classroom in physical proximity to all students.
8. Maintain an open body posture.
9. Listen attentively to what students say.
10. Call each student by name.
11. Remain calm and unflustered.

There are many resources and Web sites devoted to the topic of discipline. You can find many of these books and Web sites listed and annotated in Chapter 15. Become your own researcher and as you sub in various classrooms, keep a file of ideas related to discipline. Write down the classroom rules, collect the information the teacher provides in the sub folder, and collect policies from schools you visit. Look around the room for "points charts" and treasure boxes. This archive will serve you well in your subbing experiences and later, if you should pursue a teaching credential.

CHAPTER 12

Low-Key Interventions
and Responses to Avoid

Effectiveness Essentials

- You can deal with some minor infractions and distractions in a low-key manner.

- Effective nonverbal body language consists of teacher gestures, body posture, facial expressions, eye contact, and proximity control.

- Deal with discipline problems without overreacting and resorting to negative responses.

Whatever discipline system is in place can be augmented by the suggestions that follow. These include low-key and nonverbal interventions and responses to avoid. Although prevention is the best policy, including having rules and a commanding presence, you will still have to resort to some of these suggestions, which are used daily by the most experienced teachers.

Nonverbal and Low-Key Interventions

You can deal with minor infractions and distractions nonverbally without disrupting the entire class or instructional sequence. Effective nonverbal body language consists of teacher gestures, body posture, facial expressions, eye contact, and proximity. The suggestions that follow have no money-back guarantee that all misbehaviors can be handled without sacrificing instructional time. But try them first before resorting to harsher penalties or consequences.

Sign Language

You can learn and teach to students some simple signs in American Sign Language (ASL). You can use signs to convey nonverbal messages without disturbing the class. Also, when students use this valuable communication tool, they may develop an interest in acquiring more signs. See the Apply It! box for ways to access ASL online.

Apply It!

Go to a free website such as www.aslpro.com/cgi-bin/aslpro/aslpro.cgi that uses video to demonstrate a full dictionary of ASL terms. There you can access signs for quiet, sit down, stand up, and so forth. (See Figure 12.1.) You can also access signs simply by clicking on Google images and typing in "American Sign Language Sit." Access five other terms you may need in your classroom.

Figure 12.1 ASL Sign for "Sit" Place the palm side of the right hand fingers on the back of the left hand fingers; then move both hands down slightly.

Teacher Talks...

Years ago I had to learn some American Sign Language including the alphabet, because I was temporarily assigned a partially deaf student. Since then I've incorporated the use of some sign language to quietly communicate back and forth with my students, thus not disturbing the whole class. We communicate things like water, bathroom, recess time, lunchtime, concentrate/focus, read, write, sit down, etc. The students seem to enjoy learning the alphabet and other signs.

Gabe Aguilar
Sixth grade

The Look

The best prevention is to keep your eyes and feet moving throughout the room so you can get to trouble spots quickly and nip misbehaviors before they morph into more serious behaviors. Establishing eye contact with the offender and staring until the behavior diminishes works for some teachers. Jones (1992, 2000) advocates this practice, along with other nonverbal interventions. Remember that cultural norms may inhibit the student from looking directly back at you.

Physical Proximity

Walking toward the offender will usually stop the behavior. You may need to move closer to the student and stand nearby. The increasing invasion of the student's space will usually cause him or her to desist. A hand on the desk as you pass is also effective, if moving to the edge of the desk hasn't achieved the desired outcome. You may want to learn more about nonverbal limit setting by reading the work of Fred Jones (1992, 2000).

A Classroom Example

Sam and Maria are talking during a lesson. The substitute follows these steps:

Make eye contact and let them know they are being watched.

Give a shake of the head while maintaining eye contact.

Hold up a hand, palm outward, signaling stop.

Move toward the offenders.

Stand next to the offenders.

Put hand on desk of offenders.

Look right at them and glare.

Signals

Use signals with individuals or with the whole class. Signals that work in general are shaking the head, raising the eyebrows, a quick arc of the finger. Count down from 10 to 1 to get the students quiet or clap out a pattern they have to imitate or answer. Have a song that they can join in singing quietly. Play a few notes on the piano to settle students down. Use a bell or message on the board to alert students that you have something important to say. Turn off the lights for quiet. If you establish the proper noise level at the beginning of any activity, you will be well ahead of the game. Whatever your signal, teach it at the outset and positively reinforce the first responders.

Enlisting Cooperation

You can often nip the misbehavior in the bud by enlisting the student's aid for some small task related to the lesson. You might ask the culprit to erase the board or pass out materials. Whatever the job, both you and the offender will know why he or she has been chosen, and you still won't miss a beat in your instruction.

Questioning

Posing a question to the student who has just started to act out can redirect his or her attention to the task. Make sure it is a question that can be answered easily, as your goal is not to embarrass the student but to channel his or her attention in a productive way. If you feel the student cannot answer the question, have him or her select someone whose hand is raised to supply the answer.

The Encouraging Moment

When you observe a potential offender doing something right or trying to do the right thing, offer encouraging words. You are better off waiting for the moment when you get your chance to turn a student in the direction of success. Strike when the iron is hot and encourage your student.

"See Me" and Positive Behavior Cards

You can duplicate cards that you can unobtrusively place on a student's desk that say something equivalent to "See Me." You may also have a place for students to write in why they think they received the card and what a better choice would have been.

Positive coupons or tickets for a visit to a treasure chest work well as you walk around the room to monitor good behavior. Tickets and coupons can be part of your "Substitute Supplies."

Delayed Reaction

Rather than interrupt the flow of instruction, simply and firmly tell the student in question that you wish to speak to him or her at the end of the lesson.

Student Says...

How is a substitute teacher different from your regular teacher?

She doesn't take away WOW! tickets. She knows about them, but she doesn't take them away.

> *Drew, age 7*
> *Second grade*

This invitation to a private conference, only one sentence in length, may cause the student to shape up, negating the need for a long conference. The delayed reaction also gives you a chance to cool off and consider an appropriate response. Nelsen (2000) suggests that this cooling off is most important when you are angry or frustrated and are likely to exacerbate the situation by responding in kind to the student's discouraged behavior.

Role Playing or Letter Writing

It's often useful for students to write out their angry feelings or express their point of view in a dispute on paper. In the case of the upset student, writing it out is a more positive way of diminishing strong feelings. In a dispute the

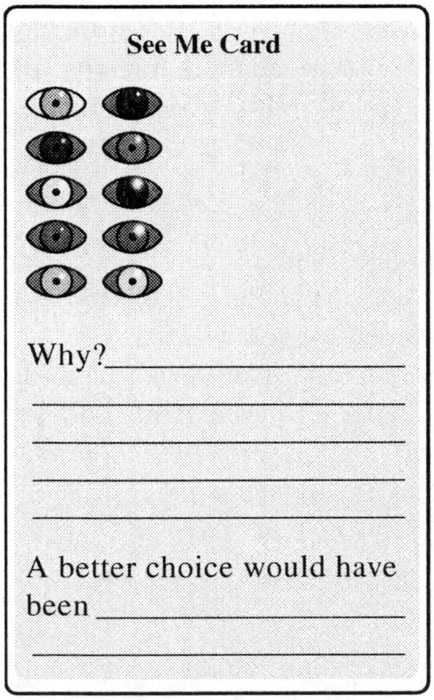

See Me Card

Why?_____

_____

_____

_____

A better choice would have been _____

_____

Figure 12.2 "See Me" Card

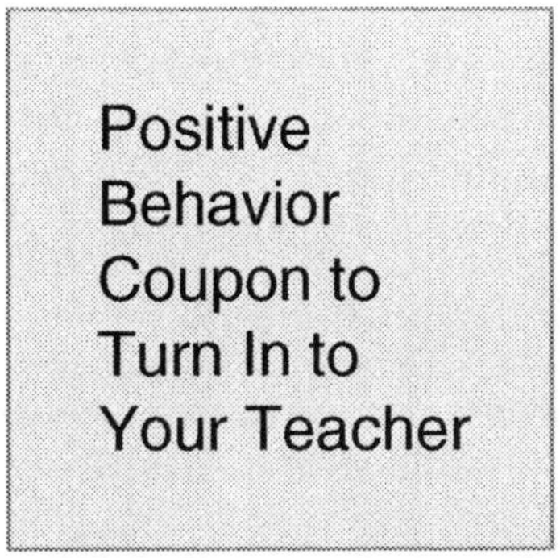

Positive
Behavior
Coupon to
Turn In to
Your Teacher

Figure 12.3 Positive Behavior Card

two students can exchange their papers and read each other's description of the events leading up to the altercation. You can position the two students on opposite sides of you and have each tell what happened from the other's point of view. This helps them to understand, if not empathize with, the other student and, thus, ameliorate the conflict. This is much more effective than asking them why they behaved badly, a question that may elicit a glib response or no response at all. What you want to ask is how they can make it right.

Make a Better Choice

Give the students a choice, either cease and desist or_____. Make it a good choice. For example, if two students are fooling around, say, "Stop socializing or I will move your seats. Make a choice." If a girl is applying makeup, tell her, "Either put the compact away or I will take it away. Make a good choice." If a youngster is rocking back and forth in a chair, say, "Either stop rocking or you may need to stand up. What you are doing is not safe, so make a good choice."

Time Out

This is a cooling-off period for the disruptive student, but the way you present it makes all the difference. Use a "thinking chair" for the young set and an isolated study carrel for older students. After you issue the "make a choice" challenge, you can isolate those who refuse to make the proper choice of desisting. Give the student a timer and set it to the appropriate amount of time; some suggest a minute for every year old. So a kindergarten student will have 5 minutes to sit out the action and a senior in high school 18 minutes or so. An in-room time out is much more effective and safer than sending the student out of the room, either to the office or another room.

Ignore Some Disruptions

You will never have a day or period of complete silence or perfect behavior. You will have to make some choices about what behavioral disruptions you can live with. You have to choose your "battles" or you will never get any teaching done. Sometimes it is best to ignore minor disruptions and go on. Other times, tell the students that you are willing to let it go if it doesn't happen again. I call this "dropping the rope."

Responses to Avoid

The hardest part of dealing with discipline problems of the more serious kind is repressing some of the very human responses that serious offenses provoke. If there is ever a time to put on your angel's wings and sit under a halo, it's when a serious offense occurs in the classroom. A calm, cool manner on your part will not only disarm the offender but will also soothe the other students, who may be as upset as you are. What follows are various responses to avoid. It is impossible to avoid all of them. But try.

Holding a Grudge and/or Taking It Personally

When the behavior has been dealt with, try to wipe the slate clean and forgive and forget. You have a long day to go and even in a short period, you want to model a mature response.

Separate yourself from the situation and realize that the behavior is symptomatic of some disturbance within the student and doesn't necessarily reflect his or her attitude toward you. This may require that you schedule frequent pep talks with yourself.

Making Everyone Suffer

It simply isn't fair to apply consequences to the entire class because a few of the students are misbehaving. Discriminate between the offenders and the nonoffenders and go on with business as usual.

Student Says...

A substitute teacher should not punish the whole class for what two or three kids did. One time a substitute teacher made the whole class miss recess when just three kids were throwing pencils. I really hate that.

Walker, age 12
Seventh grade

Ejection from the Room

It is illegal in many districts to banish students from the classroom and situate them outside the room unsupervised. Even if it is not, it is still not a good solution. Students will simply fool around in the halls or on the playground. You can be sure they won't stay where you put them. Avoid sending them to another classroom or to the principal except in rare instances. Not only does this burden the other teachers and the principal, but also, if you exercise this option too frequently, you may not be called back to sub in that classroom or school. Unfairly or not, your administrator may conclude that you cannot deal with misbehavior. Try to tough it out and deal with problems in the classroom.

Physical Contact

Corporal punishment is defined as punishment upon the body, and it is banned in many states. Although you may be driven to distraction, never grab, pinch, or hit the students. They will magnify some of the slightest restraining techniques, and you need to protect yourself from irate parents and even a lawsuit. Also, you don't want to model a physical response to the rest of the class, as you are hoping to extinguish this kind of behavior in them.

Equally, in this day and age, a harmless touch, hand on the shoulder, pat on the back, hug, or any other positive physical contact may result in claims of sexual harassment. You have to be aware of the consequences of touching a student, no matter how harmless the intent.

Yelling, Screaming, or Pleading

Yelling, screaming, and pleading will label you in the eyes of your students as unable to manage the class, and they will make a bad situation worse if they feel you are out of control. Present yourself to the students as a professional with a calm demeanor. You will need a time out yourself when you are most angry, so tell the offender that you will speak to him or her at recess or after the period ends.

Parent's Point of View...

Speaking as a parent who has listened to my kids complain about subs: get them engaged; have some activities to fill in beyond what the teacher left—something new and unexpected that is grade and subject appropriate; don't punish the whole class for the behavior of a few; don't raise your voice—yelling doesn't gain you control of the class, it just gains you more kids trying to push your buttons; be interested in the kids and try to learn something about them.

Helena Vendrzyk Gordon

Emotional objectivity, according to Marzano (2003), is a key construct of an effective classroom management plan. Emotional objectivity requires that no matter how upset you may be with a student, you continue to interact in a businesslike manner. If you are perceived as overreacting or as biased, the offender will blame you for being "prejudiced" or "making a big deal out of nothing" instead of taking responsibility. Anticipate which students might act out and then purposely talk yourself into positive expectations for the day or period.

Humiliation

Included in this category of don'ts is sarcasm, nagging, requiring the wearing of a dunce hat, having the student stand in a corner, or imposing other

> ## Former Substitute/High School Teacher Talks...

Be calm. Kids can smell fear.

Susan Johnson

public embarrassment. It also includes very negative comments to students that will only make matters worse. The students need to save face, and if you can talk with the offender privately, you are denying him or her an audience for further defiance or face-saving entrenchment of the negative behavior.

More Work

Writing sentences 25 times or more or doing extra work may not change the behavior. Rather, it may negatively associate work, which should be intrinsically pleasurable, with punishment.

Threats You Can't/Won't Carry Out

You will lose your credibility if you back down, so avoid this by thinking carefully about consequences before you announce them. Try withdrawing from the situation and establish a cooling-off period. Find a way for both of you to win if you are in a stand-off situation. Saying, "I am choosing to let that go this time, although I expect that you will be respectful to all your classmates in the future," allows you both an easy out, and you are still in control of the situation by making the choice. Or have your student choose between desisting and the logical consequence of the behavior.

Apply It!

Consider the following 10 classroom behaviors that vary in degree from minor to serious. It's better to preplan possible interventions before they actually occur! Devise a plan for dealing with these situations in elementary grades or secondary levels:

1. A student calls out or interrupts.
2. A student destroys the property of another student.
3. A student forgets her homework.
4. A student taps his pencil on the desk constantly.
5. A student says, "You can't make me."
6. A student shoves another student in line.
7. A student brings a weapon to class.
8. A student gets out of her seat and walks around the room.
9. A student threatens another student.
10. Students are noisy and won't quiet down.

Possible responses:

1. Ignore and state that you only listen to answers that are preceded by a raised hand. Or raise your own hand as a signal.
2. Student needs to make retribution (leave a note for the regular teacher) and apologize to the student whose property was defaced.
3. Write a note to the teacher and have the student try to finish sometime during the day or at lunchtime so you can tear up the note.
4. "Make a choice. Either stop or you will need to give up your pencil and use a crayon for your work."
5. Admit that this is true and encourage the student in a friendly manner to start working.
6. Have the student walk next to you and require the student to apologize to the student who was pushed.
7. Call the office immediately.
8. Ignore if the student returns to her seat or give the ASL signal for sit.
9. Remain calm and call the office immediately.
10. Use a predetermined signal, such as playing music, clapping a pattern, turning off the lights, and so on.

Principal's Perspective...

Some final words from a principal include these suggestions regarding discipline matters:

Be friendly; be cheerful.
Treat them with respect, whether or not they do the same for you!
Lose the sarcasm.
Don't awake the sleeping monster!
Circulate, circulate, circulate!
Watch, watch, watch!
Listen, listen, listen!

Dr. Virginia Newlin, NBCT

Do not worry too much about the possible disruptive behaviors you may encounter. Each day of subbing is a learning experience, and you will be a better sub with each and every day of subbing, especially in matters of discipline. If you maintain a positive attitude and remember that less is more in matters of discipline, except in cases of dangerous behaviors, you will come out of your day energized and ready for the next challenge.

CHAPTER 13

Engaging All Learners

This chapter starts with an overview of the importance of connecting with students and how to be successful despite unfamiliarity with the subjects and students you are called upon to teach, including students with special needs and those who are English learners. Finally, there are some research-based strategies that you might want to use to spice up the plans and deliver concepts and skills in a more engaging way.

Connecting with Students

The substitute teacher who conveys a positive and enthusiastic attitude will be sized up by the students as someone who is really there to save the day for learning. Do not be influenced by what the regular teacher, colleagues, or the staff tell you about the class. This can lead to a self-fulfilling prophecy. If you think that you are going to have a bad day, you will act in ways that confirm your expectations, and you probably will have one. If, on the other hand, you enter the classroom conveying that the day will go smoothly, you will reassure the students, and they will rise to your expectations.

Relate Learning to Personal Experience

Ask the students what they already know, feel, or have experienced vis-à-vis the topic. Or use a KWL (Ogle, 1986) chart to extract the prior knowledge. Divide the board or a poster into three columns. Label the first "What We Know," the second, "What We Want to Know," and the third, after instruction, "What We Learned." Before you begin a lesson ask the students to fill in the first column; for example, "What do we know about penguins?" List all their responses, and then ask them what they want to know about penguins. After reading the assigned selection, go back to the chart and check to see if the knowledge column items are true or false. Then go to the second column and check to see whether their questions were answered. Add new information to the third column.

Have Fun

You will not compromise your authority when you show true concern for your students, or even act a little goofy, or use some of your own creative ideas to implement the requisite lesson. One sub tells the high school students her name, but also tells them they can call her "Grandma." They greet her on campus with a loving, "Hi, Grandma." They tell her she is the best sub they ever had. Use some of your own experiences if they are

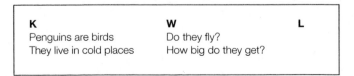

Figure 13.1 KWL Chart

Student Says...

Subs play fun games with us. Subs are nice. They are different from the regular teacher because they play different games and do different P.E. When they get in the room, they tell us their name and the first thing we are going to do. We go over the rules and all the substitutes are different from one another. Yesterday when we had a sub everybody was being bad. We played addition bingo but it wasn't as good as with the other sub. We had three different subs for three days. The first was best because she was funny and she had puppets. The puppets read the books and they talked funny and they made the sounds like they do in the movies. She had Shrek and Donkey and Dora and Diego puppets.

Ruby Mae, age 7
Second grade

relevant to the lesson. Use some easy props, such as puppets, with the younger students.

Conduct Interesting Discussions

If the plan calls for a discussion, make sure to establish the ground rules of hand raising, listening, and respecting all responses. Keep the discussion going by injecting other questions, questions that stimulate thinking beyond the factual. Ask compare and contrast questions, evaluative questions, creative questions, analytical questions, and stop before the students get fidgety or bored. A good source for designing questions based on a progression from the simply factual to the evaluative is Benjamin Bloom's Taxonomy of Educational Objectives (1964), already mentioned briefly in Chapter 8. Consider various levels of questions as you conduct your discussion.

CLASSROOM ARTIFACT

Bloom's Taxonomy of Educational Objectives, Sample Questions at Each Level

Knowledge Questions: Facts or Recall

What are the rules for basketball?
Name the characters in the story.
Name all the animals you would find in the desert.
What states border our own?

(continued)

(Continued)

Comprehension Questions: Understanding

What was the problem in the story, and how was it resolved?

Describe impressionism in your own words.

Describe the key parts of the circulatory system.

Draw a diagram of the water cycle.

Application Questions: Transfer to a New Situation

Did anything like this ever happen to you? What? Why?

If you were in a problem situation like this one, how would you have acted?

What lesson did you learn from this account and how would you apply it to your life?

How would your life be different if you couldn't use electricity for a week?

Analysis Questions: Classification/Compare and Contrast

Compare and contrast the two main characters in the story.

Classify these rock samples into metamorphic, igneous, and sedimentary.

Compare a beehive to a city.

Compare Abraham Lincoln to George Washington.

Synthesis Questions: Creative Responses

How might you change the ending of the story?

Name one character. Tell the story from this character's point of view.

How would you convince a friend that he or she should read this book?

Create a poster of an endangered animal. Use recycled materials.

Evaluation Questions: Judgment Based on Criteria

Do you think Goldilocks should have entered the bears' house? Why or why not?

Did you like the way the story ended? Why or why not?

Which character in the book would you choose for a friend? Why?

Write a letter to the editor of our newspaper about an issue that concerns you.

Concern About Content and Unfamiliar Students

Many subs avoid middle and high school at all costs because they fear that they will be clueless in geometry class, klutzy in gym class, or challenged in a computer lab. Actually, subs I know prefer the time frame of a period as opposed to the all-day, self-contained classroom found in elementary schools. While the elementary students may be easier to manage, at least the period is over quickly, and you can try something different when the new group of students arrives for the next period.

> **Retired High School Teacher/ Substitute Speaks...**

Have realistic expectations depending on the type of class you are in. The high achievers will automatically proceed on their own. Medium groups will need some additional direction. Low groups will look to you for guidance. Special education classes usually have aides who will tell you what is expected. Some classes have student assistants or aides who know exactly what to do.

The subject matter should be the least of your concerns. An example would be if you are in a French class and know nothing about the language. Be honest and say, "I speak Spanish, not French." Remember, you are there in place of the regular teacher and you will do your best to make the day productive. Write the assignment on the board. In advanced classes, students know who the most capable are and they will identify a student who can help you out. Be flexible.

Nancy DeMaggio

Apply It!

What Would You Do?

In keeping with the concerns about not being familiar with the content or subject matter, decide what you would do in each of these instances:

1. You have a physical education class of 50 students and you are not physically fit.
2. You are assigned to a continuation school and have a class of pregnant minors.
3. You have a high math class and you are mathematically challenged.
4. You are assigned to a computer lab.
5. You are assigned to a kindergarten and you have no clue about this age group.
6. You are assigned to an art class.
7. You have a gifted class of sixth-grade clowns.
8. You have a group of students with hearing impairments.

Possible courses of action with input from Nancy DeMaggio, Retired High School Teacher and Substitute:

1. Usually a couple of students will come forward and tell you the procedures. You will probably have to deal with equipment, so designate a student to take a count and then make him or her responsible for returning as many pieces of equipment as went out.
2. A continuation school is for students who require an alternative program. The classes are smaller and the students have contracts that earn them points and credits. They know what they should be doing.

3. The students will know which student "gets it" and that person can be your teaching assistant for the period. This will be like teaching in college, and the students will actually be teaching themselves.

4. In the computer lab, the students will have their assignments to work on. In the event that they don't, you can ask them to write a letter to the president, map their neighborhood, write a story and illustrate it with clip art, find a biography of their favorite sports star or historical figure, or create a PowerPoint presentation for any other class.

5. The little ones will be most anxious about their teacher's absence. They may never have experienced a sub. Tell them a little about yourself and reassure them that you have instructions from their teacher, and while you may not do things exactly the same way as Mrs. _____, it will make Mrs._____ very happy to know that "We will have a great day." Usually kindergarten and other elementary teachers are so concerned about being absent that they will have left voluminous plans, beyond what the school requires.

6. Again, the students will know what projects they are working on. In the absence of plans (unlikely), set up a still life of objects in the room and have them draw.

7. Middle school kids can be fun, and your biggest challenge will be keeping a straight face. Invite them to teach parts of the lesson and tell them that when they finish the work, they can watch a surprise DVD you have brought.

8. The hearing-impaired class will have an aide who will guide you. Make sure to write the assignments on the board in big letters, speak facing the class, and then consider learning ASL (American Sign Language) in the future.

Use common sense if you find yourself confused or bewildered in an unfamiliar setting with specialized content or students with unique needs. Remember that the teacher should have left more complete plans or instructions and that you have done your best to follow what instructions you do have. Then consider taking out your supplemental resources. Supplemental activities and materials are described in Chapter 15.

Students with Special Needs

The concept of least restrictive environment (LRE) is one you need to understand since there is a great chance that you will encounter students with special needs in a special day class, a mainstreaming situation, or an inclusion class. Least restrictive environment means that to the maximum extent appropriate, students with special needs are educated with their nondisabled peers along a continuum. That means if the students are not in all-day special classes, they will be mainstreamed for part of the day into regular classrooms to interact with peers, or they may be included in regular classrooms with an aide present to offer assistance. By law, a student with special needs has an IEP (Individualized Education Plan). The regular teacher should have left instructions for you regarding what needs to be done to accommodate the student(s). There may be special equipment like an adapted keyboard that the student uses, a magnifying device, and so on. The aide will have this information and will be a great asset to you.

Apply It!

Define and familiarize yourself with these terms:

> ADHD
> ADD
> LRE
> PL 94-142
> IEP (Individualized Education Plan)
> Special day class
> LD (learning disorder)
> SED (severely emotionally disturbed)
> Autism
> Mainstreaming
> Inclusion

In general, when you are working with several students with special needs or just one such student in a regular classroom, it is important to remember these principles:

1. Treat the student with respect, patience, flexibility, and, above all, a kind, compassionate, and gentle demeanor.
2. Make any accommodations that make sense, such as allowing more time for an assignment, giving shorter assignments, arranging for peer assistance, writing directions on the board, giving immediate feedback, encouraging small successes, and seeking help from resource teachers or the principal.
3. Learn all you can about the conditions that you encounter. There are so many conditions affecting students that it is best to learn about them slowly as you encounter them.

Working with English Language Learners

Principles of good instruction apply to the instruction of English language learners, and the task is not as formidable as you may feel. Most experts suggest that hands-on, active learning strategies work well with students learning English. Working with English learners affords you an exciting opportunity to learn about new cultures and even new languages while seeking exciting and creative ways to differentiate instruction to meet the needs of the English language learners. The ELL students are a valuable resource to the entire class, improving everyone's English language skills and cross-cultural understanding.

Most English language learners will be in immersion and sheltered English classes or regular classes. Some English learners may be enrolled in bilingual classes taught by bilingual teachers or in dual language immersion classes where a percentage of each day is spent learning in both languages, and the classes are evenly divided between English learners and native English speakers.

Sheltered English, also referred to as Specially Designed Academic Instruction in English (SDAIE), presents grade-level appropriate content in English using special techniques. In the immersion and SDAIE programs the language of instruction is English. As a sub there are some techniques you can use to enhance learning.

Eight Ways a Sub Can Promote English Language Development

1. Preview and review material graphically (concept maps, graphic organizers, Venn diagrams).
2. Incorporate substantial oral language opportunities in each lesson.
3. Use maps, graphs, props, concrete materials, visuals, photographs.
4. Dramatize content with gestures and facial expressions.
5. Model clear and understandable written and oral language.
6. Allow sufficient time for responses and discussion.
7. Give clear directions and review and summarize frequently.
8. Define new words and avoid using idioms and slang.

Help is available if you are new to these ELL strategies. Confer with teachers and resource personnel at your site or at the district level. Ask the principal for advice as needed. Ask the bilingual coordinator and other bilingual teachers to help you out. Use the translation Web site http://babelfish.altavista.com for translating simple messages to students or use bilingual peers to interpret directions for you. Read all you can about strategies for working with English learners.

Spicing Up Lessons with Researched Strategies

There are some simple, research-based techniques to spice up your lessons. You will be following the teacher's lesson plan and addressing the objective, but you will be doing so with a slight twist to make the lesson more engaging.

Concept Formation

Brainstorm with the students about what they got out of the chapter they just read or read the day before. Then write all the ideas on the board and have the students, one at a time, come up to the board and categorize the words,

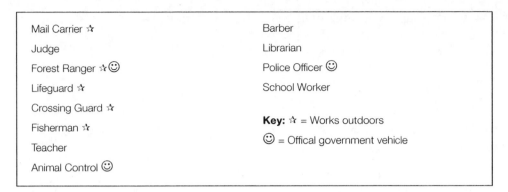

Mail Carrier ☆

Judge

Forest Ranger ☆☺

Lifeguard ☆

Crossing Guard ☆

Fisherman ☆

Teacher

Animal Control ☺

Barber

Librarian

Police Officer ☺

School Worker

Key: ☆ = Works outdoors

☺ = Offical government vehicle

Figure 13.2   Labeling Using Symbols

using symbols. (See Figure 13.2.) They need to justify why they made that grouping and then label the grouping.

Venn Diagrams and Other Graphic Organizers

Students can make a Venn diagram comparing and contrasting material in the text they have read. Venn diagrams help students compare and contrast two or more objects or ideas. They can make a list of the first element, then the second, and transfer both lists to the diagram. The common elements are listed in the overlap area. The diagrams can be used to compare and contrast two different story characters, two different stories, two historical figures, two rock samples, two mammals, and so forth.

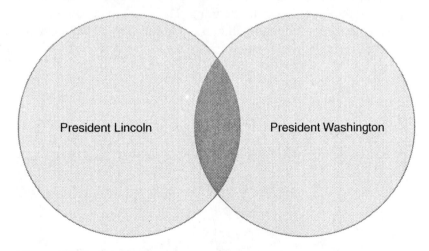

President Lincoln

President Washington

Figure 13.3   Venn Diagram

Other graphic organizers include the following:

Sequence Charts   Sequence charts help students place events in order. They can be used for:

- Time lines
- Plot sequence
- Steps in an experiment
- Project procedures
- Story boards
- Steps in problem solving
- Directions of any kind

Circular Charts   Circular charts can be used to help students visualize or depict cyclic events. Some ideas are:

- The water cycle
- The food chain
- The seasons

Concept Maps   Concept maps are another way to represent ideas in graphic form. *Kidspiration* and *Inspiration* (http://www.inspiration.com) are superb technological applications, but you can make webs on your board or on charts as well.

Cooperative Learning

In the teacher's lesson plan, he or she may indicate that the lesson is to be conducted in cooperative learning format. The procedures may be clearly outlined for you. But if you are vague on how to implement cooperative learning, here is a very simple outline of the steps:

1. First, decide on a task that can be divided evenly into three or four equal parts. An example would be story editing. The jobs might be Punctuation Editor, Capitalization Editor, Spelling Editor, and Overall Organization Editor. Clearly explain and demonstrate what each job is about.

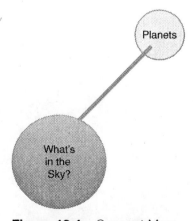

Figure 13.4   Concept Map

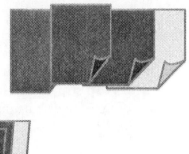

Figure 13.5 Cooperative Learning Tools

2. Denote which jobs are which using color-coded papers and "tickets." You can change the key for different cooperative learning tasks each time, reusing the papers and tickets.

3. Hand out the tickets to groups of four and have students choose a color that is coded to the job they want. If they can't decide in three minutes, you will decide for them.

4. Set a time limit and announce a social skill, such as talking softly, saying please or thank you, sharing materials, calling one another by name, listening, and so on.

5. Monitor the groups and check to see that the groups are using the skill.

6. Review with the students how things went, and have them fill out an evaluation of their participation, use of skill, and so on.

CLASSROOM ARTIFACT

High School English Cooperative Learning Lesson Plan

After input and a test on poetic devices and figurative language, I assign each student one poem. I group the poems according to theme: love, death, war, nature, etc. Each group (four or five in a group) discusses all the poems in their group to determine what theme they all have in common. They also must decide how each poet treats the theme differently and come up with reasons why.

Then each group presents their poems and leads the class in a discussion. They are required to read their poems aloud and use some kind of visual aid. (One group wore berets and brought in real coffee for a coffeehouse setting.) After all groups are finished, each student writes a critical analysis of his or her poem.

When finished, each student has studied his or her own poem in great depth, the poems in his or her group in some depth, and all the other poems in the class briefly.

Susan Johnson
Advanced Placement English and language arts

Reciprocal Teaching

Reciprocal teaching (Palincsar, 1984) is very similar to cooperative learning, and it can spice up any lesson that involves reading text material. Reciprocal teaching lends itself to very clearly defined roles and procedures. In fact, it is so structured that you might try this strategy as your initiation into cooperative learning before you try anything more complex.

1. Group students (four per group).
2. Identify students in each group for each of the four roles for the first round:
     i. Summarizer
    ii. Questioner
   iii. Clarifier
    iv. Predictor
3. Students read _____ paragraphs and utilize note-taking strategies.
4. The Summarizer draws attention to the key ideas.
5. The Questioner poses questions regarding the selection.
6. The Clarifier addresses puzzling elements and tries to answer the questions that were posed.
7. The Predictor offers guesses about what comes next.
8. Repeat the process for the next _____ paragraphs, switching roles to the right or left.

Apply It!

Try out a reciprocal teaching lesson. Use the textbooks as the source of reading material. Model each and every step along the way before you set the students to the task. Have the students read along with you. Act out each of the four roles yourself, modeling what kind of statements or questions each group member is likely to ask or state. Check for understanding by having the students practice each role separately while you give feedback. Then let them get into their groups, assign a short text passage, set a time limit, and let them go for it. Monitor them and provide corrective feedback if needed. Debrief them and discuss any problems they encountered.

If your teacher has stated that the students are to read any text material, you can use any of the strategies to liven up the reading.

Finally, do your best to follow the teacher's lesson plans, and as you implement the lessons, the tips in this chapter will help you expand your own repertoire and make the day more productive and exciting for you and your "temporary" students.

CHAPTER 14

Ending the Day and Relaxing

At the end of a successful day of subbing there are a few more responsibilities you need to assume so you can make a good impression. They involve ending the day or period with the students on a positive note, making sure that you leave the room cleaner and more orderly than you found it, and, finally, finding time to unwind and relax after a full day of subbing.

Ending the Day or Period

Closure is important at the end of the day. Look for directions on ending the day in the sub folder. If you do not find this information in written form somewhere, ask a "reliable" student or nearby colleague what the procedures are at the end of the day. If you still have no apparent directions, use the following suggestions.

Elementary Grades

Set a timer or use an alarm clock (bring these with you) to remind you and the students that it is time to clean up. Use the last 5–10 minutes for a quick review of the day's activities with the students, discussing what they learned or enjoyed most that day. Use the time for clearing off desks, cleaning out desks, tidying up the room, and making sure that all papers and notices that need to go home are distributed. Buses run on schedules, and they can't wait for students to clean up. Offer a special, individualized, and positive comment to as many students as time allows as you dismiss them.

Middle and High School

Many of the same routines for ending the day also pertain to ending the period in middle and high schools. You can set a timer, and when it rings, have the students clean up, gather their papers, make sure they have copied the homework, summarize the lesson, and review the homework. If you have time you can ask them to tell you what was most interesting, what idea was completely new to them, ask any remaining questions, predict what they will learn the next period, and so on.

Remember that *you* signal the end of the period—*not* the bell. In high school, the last-period teacher, especially at the end of the week, has the biggest challenge corralling the students who are antsy to get to after-school jobs, practices, pep rallies, games, or just get home. You will need to plan accordingly for those last 10 minutes of the final period of the day and the week. You can make copies of this middle/high school period evaluation form for the students to fill out. They can do this quickly and your teacher will be grateful for the specific feedback.

High School Period Evaluation Form for Substitutes

Subject_____ Date_____ Period_____ Teacher_____

What were the 3 most important things you learned today?

What questions do you still have?

What will you do to resolve these questions?

Do you have any suggestions for improving the lesson?

Figure 14.1   Evaluation Form

Apply It!

A pleasant way to end each day is the compliment activity. Randomly distribute the nametags, index cards, or sticks you used to call on students (Chapter 9). Everyone in turn compliments the student whose name they receive. Thus, everyone gets and gives a compliment. For example, Miguel gets Steve's stick or card and says, "I would like to compliment Steve for. . . ." Steve says "thank you" and then gives the next compliment to the person whose name he has been given. And so on. In this way, the students leave school with a positive outlook for the next day.

Teacher Talks...

Regardless of how your day has gone, before students leave, give positive affirmations either to the whole class or to individuals. Students leave the classroom with positive feelings.

Marsha Moyer
Third grade

Use the following checklist to ensure that your end of the day or end of the period is as smooth as the beginning.

✓ Set a timer for at least 5-10 minutes before the day is over.
✓ Ask the students what the cleanup procedures are and follow them.
✓ Collect all books and materials.
✓ If you have promised rewards from a treasure box, make sure to exchange reward "tickets" for prizes.
✓ Remind students of the homework assignment.

✓ Have students clean out their desks/pass the wastebasket.

✓ Wipe down desks to make an even better impression.

✓ Compliment the students for a productive day or period.

✓ Have them put their chairs up if that is the routine.

✓ Have the students line up by bus, walkers, parents/sibling pick-ups and so forth.

✓ Wish them a good afternoon or rest of day as they leave.

After the Students Are Dismissed

After the students leave, you will either fill out a form that the teacher has provided for you or you can write a note to the teacher. There is a divided opinion on how much "bad" news to include in the note. As you read these responses, first from a principal, then from a high school sub, and lastly from an elementary sub, you will note that they differ in their approaches.

Principal's Perspective...

Follow the instructions left by the teacher as carefully as possible. Nothing annoys a teacher more than to find a substitute has not covered the material as instructed and, as a result, he or she has to make up lost instructional time. What does the regular teacher want to know?

- *Were students able to complete everything assigned?*
- *Names and actions of particularly troublesome students*
- *Amount of effort students put into their work*

Dr. Virginia Newlin, NBCT

Retired High School Teacher/ Substitute Speaks...

At the end of the day, a short note to the teacher is appreciated. "Enjoyed the day with your class" or "Most students were very cooperative." Emphasize the positive. You will be requested again!

Nancy DeMaggio

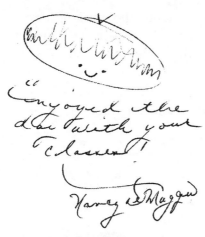

Figure 14.2 Substitute's Note

This is the note that the substitute teacher, Nancy DeMaggio, leaves for the regular teacher.

Substitute Speaks...

Leave good notes. Don't just leave a sticky note that says, "Hey, the day was okay" because that isn't going to cut it. If you had problems with a particular student, let the teacher know. If you had a student who was just really helpful and well behaved, let the teacher know. Teachers want to know that they are leaving their students in capable hands and if there are any problems that need to be addressed. Because of my notes, I have actually received an entire envelope full of apology letters from the classroom for their rude behavior when I was subbing.

Renee Zerbel

Apply It!

Compare and contrast these points of view. Is there a way to have it both ways? What is your experience, if any, with writing notes at the end of the day?

And the Cutest Note of All...

The last time I had a sub, she left a short note: "Day went fine. Kids were good. Had a visitor, though, a mouse in the sink!" The kids had some good stories to tell after that one.

Brandi Stephens
Fourth grade

Whether you leave notations about troublesome students or not, any note should include what you accomplished, checking off those items on the plan. You may want to identify especially helpful students and then note the absent students, the tardy ones, and the one who left early because of illness.

Some teachers will leave you a form to fill out at the end of the day. It has this basic information and may look like the one in Figure 14.3.

Substitute Teacher Feedback Form Provided by the School

Name_____ Subbing for_____

Grade_____ Subjects/Periods_____

Make notations on how much you covered in each period or during the day right on the lesson plan.

Comments:

Absent

Late

Taken Ill

Helpful Students

Other Comments

Teacher's e-mail _____

or

phone number_____

Figure 14.3 Feedback Form

Use paper clips to fasten like papers/assignments together and use sticky notes to identify what's in the stack. Return supplies to their proper place and check out the room to see that it is even neater than you found it.

Take some photos of the bulletin boards that appeal to you for future reference as well as any copies of worksheets and other ideas gleaned from your day. These may come in handy in other assignments or when you are a full-time teacher.

In the office, turn in your key, and fill in any paperwork so you can get paid. Thank the school secretary and principal and tell them how much you enjoyed your day.

A Sub's Homework

After you arrive home, take some time to reflect on your day. Included in this section are some ideas for analyzing your practice and using stress and time management techniques to make your next subbing assignment even more productive.

Reflecting on the Day

Jot down your feelings, your successes, your questions, and ruminations about the day, every day you sub, in a journal you use for just this purpose. Use the following sentence stems to get started.

Apply It!

The best three things about this day were . . .

This day could have been better if . . .

I could have used more . . .

I could have used less . . .

The most interesting part of the day was . . .

The most boring part of the day was . . .

In your reflection journal, list at least 10 qualities, skills, or attitudes that make you an effective substitute teacher. Don't be shy! Then write down five areas that you would like to strengthen. Don't be shy here either. What alternatives have you considered? Write these down as well.

Never put yourself down. Even if you have had a very bad day, you need to focus on what went right and how you can ameliorate any problems the next time you sub. Substitute teachers have an opportunity to start fresh with each assignment.

Destressing and Relaxing

The hardest stress of subbing is not knowing when you will be called, what grade level or subject you will be teaching, or whether it will be a school that you are familiar with. Also, it may be difficult to plan your week if you do not have any idea which days will be sub days. You sit at home waiting for the call, and all of sudden you have to mobilize yourself, pack a lunch, and get out the door as if the house is on fire.

In the first few years of subbing, it's not at all unusual to feel anxious and to wonder how you will juggle every personal and professional demand. Balancing all your responsibilities while also establishing yourself at one or more schools takes time and can be stressful. You may be a college student, or a parent with child-care concerns, or a military spouse alone after deployment. I can assure you that, with experience, coping with the demands on your time does get better.

Give yourself time between leaving your sub assignment and arriving home to unwind, or take a few minutes upon arrival to make the transition. Your personal stress busters are unique to you. They might include taking in a movie, going to the gym, playing computer games, or listening to music.

Respecting Yourself and Your Role

One of the most important things you can do to keep stress at bay is to maintain a healthy perspective about your work. You can do your part to promote respect for substitute teachers.

1. Set realistic expectations for your role as a sub.
2. Counter any sense of isolation by socializing during lunch and recess.
3. Students appreciate substitutes with a sense of humor. Use your sense of humor to relieve any tension in the classroom and your own stress level.
4. Do some fun things with elementary kids like jumping rope or playing basketball at recess. Bring in a Frisbee and toss it around with them.

Saving time at home is key to your mental and emotional health. At home try to implement steps to conserve time for such important activities as sleeping, exercising, preparing a healthy meal, spending time with your family and friends, or just taking some time for yourself. Time management is dependent on organization.

Organize, Organize, Organize!

Find a place in your home or apartment for all of your sub-related papers, ideas, and supplemental materials. Prepare a cloth tote bag for each grade level or subject you may be called to sub in. On the way out the door, pick up the appropriate bag. This preparation relieves the stress of generating or gathering materials at the last minute. In the next and final chapter there are

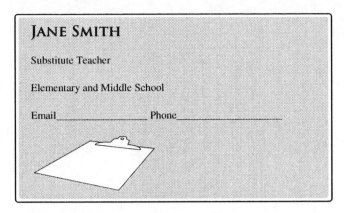

Figure 14.4   Sample Business Card

ideas for collecting your own needed materials and supplies. If you are well prepared for any situation, like an ER doctor, you will relieve much of the stress of the unknown.

Avoid comparing yourself to experienced teachers if you are new to subbing. Even though you may never have taught, you are a teacher now, a stand-in, a surrogate, a replacement, but still a teacher. Be proud of your role and perhaps make up business cards to proclaim your important role.

CHAPTER 15

Substitute Teaching Resources and Supplemental Materials

Every substitute teacher I have talked to tells me that the most stressful part of the job is the shock of not finding lesson plans. Although conscientious teachers make sub plans an essential part of their preparation for a sick day, in-service day, conference attendance, medical or family emergency, and personal day, you may encounter a situation that requires quick thinking on your part. In this chapter you will find simple solutions when you are left high and dry after finding no plans in the room or in the office where emergency plans may be kept.

Preparing for the Worst-Case Scenarios

The more prepared you are for the possibility of no plans, vague plans, or insufficient plans, the more secure you will feel. And the resources found in this chapter will be useful as supplemental materials in the event that you have time to spare after fully implementing the teacher's plans.

Retired Teacher Talks...

The substitute needs to bring some filler lessons in case there is time to fill. I would prepare a bag with several read-aloud books, games, songs, rhymes to use whenever there is time to use up. Not keeping students busy can lead to discipline problems.

Joan Smith
Reading specialist

Prepare a resource tote for grade clusters, perhaps K–1, 2–3, 4–5, middle school, high school. Your tote should include engaging lesson plans, curriculum-related puzzles, worksheets, books, crafts, and the like.

Use Your Own Background and Interests

If you have visited some exotic or historic locale, talk to the students about it. Show some artifacts and lead a discussion. If you have a talent such as playing guitar, bring your instrument along. If you have a craft like scrapbooking or quilting, share your work with the class. If you are a folk dancer, teach the class some dances from your repertoire. If you have served in the military, share your experiences and pull down the map or take out the globe and show the students where in the world you were stationed. If you have lived in another country, share your memories. If you own a horse, bring in photos of the different breeds, some tack, and some horse grooming items. If you have an uncommon plant at home, bring it in and share its name, botanical name, have the students draw it, and so on.

> ### Retired High School Teacher/ Substitute Speaks...

In certain assignments you can utilize your own talent if necessary like playing the piano, knitting, and discussing sports and current events. Working on crosswords, jumble puzzles, Sudoku are just a few activities which can provide enrichment. Asking students to write a letter to their grandparents gets their attention. Some of the suggestions are very useful if lesson plans are totally inadequate.

Nancy DeMaggio

Apply It!

Think about your own skills and talents. What could you bring to the classroom that has meaning for you and would be of interest to the students?

Use Web Resources

The first place to start is www.lessonplanspage.com. Here you will find free, downloadable lesson plans, worksheets, activities, and the like. You choose the subject and then choose the grade level, and you are good to go. Another site that will provide you with more ideas and lessons than you can use is www.edhelper.com. Here you will find puzzles, word searches, crosswords, daily themed units, Sudoku, lesson plans, and activities. These are not the only Web sites available. Use Google to identify other sites that offer teacher resources. There is a list of other sites at the end of the chapter.

Use the Local Newspaper

The daily newspaper can provide multiple materials for students. For example, cut out the crosswords, scrambles, word searches, and Sudoku puzzles and keep them in a file. Bring the paper to class and have the students choose an article to summarize. Cut off the headlines of articles and have the students write their own. Hand out an article and have the students circle all the words they don't know, and then have them look up the words and use at least five of them in a paragraph. Or just provide newspaper photos and let the students create the stories.

For younger students, give out newspaper ads and have them create a dinner for under $8.00 for a family of four. Or have them create a wish list of birthday toys from ads. Have the primary students circle all the nouns in a story. Have students look for movie ads and write a review. Have students look up favorite team stats and make up math problems. Ask the students to write to a government official about a concern. Have students interpret editorial cartoons. Cut up cartoons and let the students determine the sequence. Use any maps in the newspaper to have students do further research and identify continents, major rivers, major geographic features. The possibilities are endless.

Use Story Motivators in Class

Start collecting interesting photos from magazines for writing prompts. Bring in some of your own photos and have students write about where they were taken and what was happening at the time. Bring in an unusual object and have the students write what they think it is and how it is used. Also, develop a list of story starters, such as the following:

1. The worst day of my life was when . . .
2. My wish for the world is . . .
3. The most important person in my life is . . .
4. My perfect vacation would be . . .
5. The best birthday present would be . . .
6. My hero is . . .
7. If I made a movie, it would be about . . .
8. The best pet is . . .
9. My favorite food is . . .
10. The best baseball (basketball, soccer, football) player of all time is . . .
11. The happiest day of my life was . . .
12. When I am an adult, I want to . . .
13. My favorite TV program is . . .
14. My favorite music group or music star is . . .
15. If I were a millionaire . . .

Use Literature to Motivate Discussion or Writing

Read a story (without the title) to the students and have them provide one, or have them add a character to the story, or change the setting, or make up a different ending. This can be done in oral or written form. Have them write a review of the story, make a poster to advertise the story, or have them write to the author.

Elementary Grade Ideas

Include in your generic "sub tub" for the young set some puppets to tell the stories or lead the discussion, sing-along CDs, exercise DVDs for the primary grades, markers, crayons, small rewards for your own treasure box, and a roll of "raffle" tickets to give out for good behavior. These go into a

Teacher Talks...

A good sub, in my opinion, has to have common sense. If the written plan is not working, change it. I recently had a sub tell me she got in trouble because she was a sub in P.E. and the plan required her to play dodge ball. Students kept getting hurt, she felt a loss of control, and the principal reprimanded her for not using common sense. This can keep a sub from being called back. Also, several of our regular subs carry a "Sub Tub" with them filled with emergency tools like videos, games, and worksheets. This works great in the situations when there is not a plan or they complete the plan early. Also, the subs I call back are the ones who write me a short note about the class with their contact information on it and keep my desk clean.

Cindy Martin, NBCT
Primary grades

jar and are drawn at the end of the day for a chance to select some trinket from your treasure box. Bring a simple craft project like paper-bag puppets that they can complete in a short time. Buy some stickers and even some rubber "good work" stamps and a stamp pad.

Principal's Perspective...

Always carry along a bag of tricks, just in case! (There is a good reason for the phrase "Idle hands are the devil's playground!")

- A read-aloud book (geared to the appropriate age)
- Sponge activities to fill in activities in case the lesson is not long enough
- Ideas for indoor games:
  - Silent Softball (student who misses, throws too hard, or makes noise must sit down)
  - Simon Says
  - Question Catch: student must throw a ball to another and ask a content-related question that the catcher must answer
- Plain paper (or color by number puzzles) and colored markers. Most students like to color.
- One-page puzzles and brainteasers for those who finish early
- Sudokus are great for older kids. Younger kids like the follow-the-number puzzles (and they can color them when they finish!). Most kids also like word searches.
- Any of the How to Draw books

Dr. Virginia Newlin, NBCT

Middle and High School Ideas

Here are some ideas that are a little different from the elementary school suggestions, but there is a great deal of overlap.

- Word searches, Sudoku, crosswords, mazes, codes (a number corresponds to a letter)
- Glitter and special markers
- Magazines
- Short stories, book of poems
- Board games, such as checkers and chess
- Good work/good behavior coupons to present to their teacher
- Blank transparencies and markers in case you can't find them in the classroom
- Age-appropriate read-aloud books
- Books of riddles and jokes
- Mad-Libs

Your Own Personal Survival Kit

Don't leave home without your own personal survival kit that includes such items as:

- ✓ Map and directions to the school
- ✓ Info on starting and ending time
- ✓ Snack and lunch
- ✓ Hand sanitizer
- ✓ Sunblock and hat for outdoor activities
- ✓ Sweater
- ✓ Smock if called in for art class or primary grades
- ✓ Whistle for recess or P.E.
- ✓ Kitchen timer or alarm clock to signal cleanup time
- ✓ Umbrella
- ✓ Water bottle
- ✓ Comfortable shoes
- ✓ Change for the vending machines
- ✓ Your own pocket or electronic organizer
- ✓ Cell phone
- ✓ Meds and headache remedy
- ✓ Personal hygiene items
- ✓ Sewing kit
- ✓ Extra pair of hose
- ✓ Travel toothbrush, paste and mouthwash

Ideas for Using Vague Plans

If you have no idea what the teacher means, ask the students what they did yesterday and continue on with a review. Or you can have them make up test questions on the material, or quiz one another using the text. Conduct a discussion on the material by asking the questions in the teacher's edition.

The most motivating review strategy is the game of Jeopardy, played by two teams. You can find a Jeopardy board setup at http://jeopardylabs .com, where templates are free and sample Jeopardy games are available. There are many other sites that use PowerPoint for generating games. The students make up the questions and answers and enter them into the templates.

Students can use regular index cards, the answer on the facing side and the question on the reverse. These are pinned up on the bulletin board after they have been divided into categories and assigned monetary values. You can serve as emcee, giving the answers while teams come up with the corresponding question.

Students can also make flash cards with questions to review the subject matter, and ask one another the questions in pairs. Then the pairs exchange flash cards with another pair and try their hand at answering the questions. The question is on one side and the answer on the other.

Other game formats to review material are tic-tac-toe, baseball, or bees to review vocabulary, spelling words, or math facts. You simply draw a diagram on the board for tic-tac-toe, football, or baseball and the students define words, or spell a word correctly, or give a correct response to math facts, or review questions before they can "move." Also, the old-fashioned spelling bee is always fun. (See Figure 15.2.)

100	100	100	100	100	100
200	200	200	200	200	200
300	300	300	300	300	300
400	400	400	400	400	400
500	500	500	500	500	500

Figure 15.1 Sample Jeopardy Game

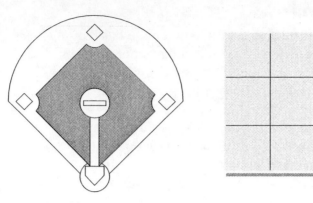
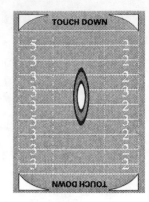

Figure 15.2 Other Game Formats

Ideas for Filling Time

Use "sponge" activities as time fillers. It's hard to think on your feet if you have an extra few minutes after you complete a lesson. Sponge activities are so named because they absorb the extra few minutes. If you don't have something to keep students actively involved, they may create their own diversions, ones you may not approve. Sponges should relate to the curriculum, call for oral responses, and require no preparation on your part. Some ideas for sponges are the following:

> Name things that come in pairs.
>
> List one country for each letter of the alphabet.
>
> Name things that fly.
>
> Name solid geometry figures.
>
> Name characters in *Romeo and Juliet.*
>
> Name the constellations.
>
> Name rights guaranteed in the Bill of Rights.
>
> Name the impressionists.
>
> Name the Greek/Roman gods and goddesses.
>
> Name the states in alphabetical order.

Apply It!

Given a grade level or subject matter you might encounter as a sub, list at least 10 sponge ideas you could use to soak up extra time.

Some Key Resources

This section of the chapter provides you with some resources that extend the information in this book. Included are a listing of state departments of education on the Web so you can contact the state you will be subbing in to find out the requirements, how to apply, and what positions may be available.

Next, you will find Web resources that will be useful to you as you prepare for the eventuality of having either no lesson plans or vague and/or limited ones. Finally, there is a list of books you may want to get from the library or purchase for your "sub tub."

State Departments of Education Online

The National Education Association (www.nea.org/home/14813.htm) provides a state-by-state status summary of the requirements, pay, and need for subs. Check out this invaluable Web site first and then go to the Web sites of the states that you are considering for employment as a sub.

State	Web Site
Alabama Department of Education	www.alsde.edu/html/home.asp
Alaska Department of Education and Early Development	www.eed.state.ak.us/
American Samoa Department of Education	www.doe.as/
Arizona Department of Education	www.ade.az.gov/
Arkansas Department of Education	arkedu.state.ar.us/
California Department of Education	www.cde.ca.gov/
Colorado Department of Education	www.cde.state.co.us/
Connecticut Department of Education	www.state.ct.us/sde/
Delaware Department of Education	www.doe.state.de.us/
District of Columbia Public Schools	www.k12.dc.us/dcps/home.html
Florida Department of Education	www.fldoe.org/
Georgia Department of Education	www.doe.k12.ga.us/index.asp
Guam Public School System	www.gdoe.net/
Hawaii Department of Education	www.k12.hi.us/
Idaho Department of Education	www.sde.state.id.us/Dept/
Illinois State Board of Education	www.isbe.net/

(continued)

State	Web Site
Indiana Department of Education	www.doe.state.in.us/
Iowa Department of Education	www.state.ia.us/educate/
Kansas Department of Education	www.ksde.org/
Kentucky Department of Education	www.kentuckyschools.org/
Louisiana Department of Education	www.louisianaschools.net/lde/index.html
Maine Department of Education	www.state.me.us/education/homepage.htm
Maryland Department of Education	www.msde.state.md.us/
Massachusetts Department of Education	www.doe.mass.edu/
Michigan Department of Education	www.michigan.gov/mde/
Minnesota Department of Education	http://education.state.mn.us
Mississippi State Department of Education	www.mde.k12.ms.us/
Missouri Department of Elementary and Secondary Education	http://dese.mo.gov/
Montana Office of Public Instruction	www.opi.state.mt.us/
Nebraska Department of Education	www.nde.state.ne.us/
Nevada Department of Education	www.doe.nv.gov
New Hampshire Department of Education	www.ed.state.nh.us/
New Jersey Department of Education	www.state.nj.us/education/
New Mexico Public Education Department	www.ped.state.nm.us/
New York Education Department	www.nysed.gov/
North Carolina Department of Public Instruction	www.ncpublicschools.org/
North Dakota Department of Public Instruction	www.dpi.state.nd.us/
Ohio Department of Education	www.ode.state.oh.us/
Oklahoma State Department of Education	http://sde.state.ok.us/
Oregon Department of Education	www.ode.state.or.us/
Pennsylvania Department of Education	www.pde.state.pa.us/
Puerto Rico Department of Education	www.de.gobierno.pr/EDUPortal/default.htm
Rhode Island Department of Elementary and Secondary Education	www.ridoe.net/
South Carolina Department of Education	http://ed.sc.gov/

State	Web Site
South Dakota Department of Education	http://doe.sd.gov/
Tennessee State Department of Education	www.state.tn.us/education/
Texas Education Agency	www.tea.state.tx.us/
U.S. Department of Education	www.ed.gov
Utah State Office of Education	www.schools.utah.gov/
Vermont Department of Education	www.state.vt.us/educ/
Virgin Islands Department of Education	www.usvi.org/education/
Virginia Department of Education	www.doe.virginia.gov/
Washington—Office of Superintendent of Public Instruction	www.k12.wa.us/
West Virginia Department of Education	wvde.state.wv.us/
Wisconsin Department of Public Instruction	www.dpi.state.wi.us/
Wyoming Department of Education	www.k12.wy.us/

Other Useful Web Sites

Discovery School's Puzzle Maker—generate customized puzzles online at http://puzzlemaker.school.discovery.com/.

Activities related to news, money, sports, or life presented by USA Today Education: www.usatoday.com/educate/substituteteachers/index.htm.

This Web site provides reading comprehension, vocabulary, geography, and other lessons: http://edhelper.com.

Education World provides lesson plans, professional development, and a special section on subbing and all the resources you will need: www.education-world.com/.

Sub Station at Education World: www.education-world.com/a_curr/curr359.shtml.

KidzOnline—you can browse for lesson plans by subject and grade: www.kidzonline.org/LessonPlans.

Lesson Plans Page—here you can find free, downloadable plans and activities in every subject and grade level: www.lessonplanspage.com

The Teachers Net/Substitute Teaching—here you can get very good ideas for subbing, including lesson plans: www.teachers.net/mentors/substitute_teaching.

University of Utah Substitute Teaching site provides tips, newsletters, and resources for subs: STEDI (Substitute Teachers Educational Development Institute), http://stedi.org/.

Works4Me Tips Library—archive of classroom tips on a variety of subjects, offered by the National Education Association: www.nea.org/helpfrom/growing/works4me/relate/subs.html.

Teach-nology provides access to lesson plans, ideas, worksheets, and much more: http://teach-nology.com/.

At ABC Teach you can find thousands of ideas and activities for elementary and middle school grades: www.abcteach.com.

A to Z Teacher Stuff has lesson plans, thematic ideas, a worksheet generator, and much, much more: www.atozteacherstuff.com.

Fun Brain offers a large collection of homemade quizzes, flash cards, and games: www.funbrain.com/teachers.

Books to Read Aloud

Hey! Listen to This: Stories to Read Aloud, ed. Jim Trelease, for ages 5–9.

Read About It!: Great Read-Aloud Stories, Poems, and Newspaper Pieces for Preteens and Teens, ed. Jim Trelease. Forty-eight works from newspapers, magazines, and books.

The 20th-Century Children's Book Treasury: Picture Books and Stories to Read Aloud by Janet Schulman.

Chicken Soup for the Kid's Soul 2: Read Aloud or Read Alone Character-Building Stories for Kids Ages 6–10 (Chicken Soup for the Soul) by Jack Canfield, Mark Victor Hansen, Patty Hansen, and Irene Dunlap.

Chicken Soup for the Soul in the Classroom—Middle School Edition: Lesson Plans and Students' Favorite Stories for Reading Comprehension, Writing Skills, Critical Thinking, Character Building by Jack Canfield, Mark Victor Hansen, and Anna Unkovich.

EPILOGUE

When I look at the children, I try to remember that the time in my classroom might be the brightest spot of their entire week. I might be the one person who says something to give them hope to combat all that is against them, the one person who can help them aim higher. I look for abilities, aspirations, talents, and dreams that will capture their dreams and compel them to give to life and take from life all possible. A few individual moments, honest compliments, and encouragement are tremendous tools.

The regular teachers often need reinforcement. I look for evidence of good things happening in the classroom and leave a positive note recognizing their efforts and commending them.

Being a sub is much more than maintaining discipline, completing worksheets, filling a teaching slot, and collecting some pay. Subbing is an opportunity to contribute to the learning of children, the betterment of the teaching staff, and the forming of bonds that build all of us.

Betty Rosentrater
Longtime teacher, K–12 in the U.S. and international
schools, and current substitute teacher at 82.

REFERENCES

Bloom, B., Mesia, B., & Krathwohl, D. (1964). *Taxonomy of educational objectives: The affective domain and the cognitive domain.* New York: David McKay.

Canter, L., & Canter, M. (2001). *Assertive discipline: Positive behavior management for today's classroom* (3rd ed.). Santa Monica, CA: Canter & Associates.

Dreikurs, R., Grunwald, B., & Pepper, F. (1998). *Maintaining sanity in the classroom* (2nd ed.). Philadelphia: Taylor and Francis.

Gardner, H. (1993). *Multiple intelligences: The theory in practice.* New York: Basic Books.

Honawar, V. (2007). Policies allow districts to cut corners with substitutes. *Education Week, 27,* 10.

House of Representatives. (2009). H.R. 2011. Substitute Teaching Improvement Act Findings. Introduced by Mr. Payne and referred to the Committee on Education and Labor, April 21, 2009. [Online] www.govtrack.us/congress/billtext.xpd?bill=h111-2011. Retrieved November 11, 2009.

Jones, F. (1992). *Positive classroom discipline.* New York: McGraw-Hill.

Jones, F. (2000). *Tools for teaching.* Santa Cruz, CA: Fred Jones & Associates.

Kounin, J. (1971; 1977). *Discipline and group management in classrooms.* New York: Holt, Rinehart and Winston.

Marzano, R., Marzano, J., & Pickering, D. (2003). *Classroom management that works.* Alexandria, VA: Association for Supervision and Curriculum Development.

Nelsen, J., et al. (2000). *Positive discipline in the classroom* (3rd rev. ed.). Roseville, CA: Prima Publishing.

Ogle, D. S. (1986). K-W-L group instructional strategy. In A. S. Palincsar, D. S. Ogle, B. F. Jones, & E. G. Carr (Eds.), *Teaching reading as thinking* (Teleconference Resource Guide, pp. 11–17). Alexandria, VA: Association for Supervision and Curriculum Development.

Palincsar, A. (1984). *Teaching reading as thinking.* Alexandria, VA: Association for Supervision and Curriculum Development.

U.S. Department of Education. (2002). *No Child Left Behind.* [Online] www.nochildleftbehind.gov/start/facts/teachers.html. Retrieved November 19, 2009.

INDEX